Autobiography of Jesse H. Pomeroy, Written by Him While Imprisoned in the Suffolk County Jail and Under Sentence of Death for The Murder of H.H. Millen

Anonymous

Autobiography of Jesse H. Pomeroy, Written by Him While Imprisoned in the Suffolk County Jail and Under Sentence of Death for The Murder of H.H. Millen

Autobiography of Jesse H. Pomeroy, Together with a sketch of his trial, the several crimes with which he is charged, and an account of his recent attempt to break jail - 1875
HAR06081
Monograph
Harvard Law School Library
Boston: Published by J.A. Cummings & Co., 248 Washington Street, 1875

The Making of Modern Law collection of legal archives constitutes a genuine revolution in historical legal research because it opens up a wealth of rare and previously inaccessible sources in legal, constitutional, administrative, political, cultural, intellectual, and social history. This unique collection consists of three extensive archives that provide insight into more than 300 years of American and British history. These collections include:

Legal Treatises, 1800-1926: over 20,000 legal treatises provide a comprehensive collection in legal history, business and economics, politics and government.

Trials, 1600-1926: nearly 10,000 titles reveal the drama of famous, infamous, and obscure courtroom cases in America and the British Empire across three centuries.

Primary Sources, 1620-1926: includes reports, statutes and regulations in American history, including early state codes, municipal ordinances, constitutional conventions and compilations, and law dictionaries.

These archives provide a unique research tool for tracking the development of our modern legal system and how it has affected our culture, government, business – nearly every aspect of our everyday life. For the first time, these high-quality digital scans of original works are available via print-on-demand, making them readily accessible to libraries, students, independent scholars, and readers of all ages.

The BiblioLife Network

This project was made possible in part by the BiblioLife Network (BLN), a project aimed at addressing some of the huge challenges facing book preservationists around the world. The BLN includes libraries, library networks, archives, subject matter experts, online communities and library service providers. We believe every book ever published should be available as a high-quality print reproduction; printed on-demand anywhere in the world. This insures the ongoing accessibility of the content and helps generate sustainable revenue for the libraries and organizations that work to preserve these important materials.

The following book is in the "public domain" and represents an authentic reproduction of the text as printed by the original publisher. While we have attempted to accurately maintain the integrity of the original work, there are sometimes problems with the original work or the micro-film from which the books were digitized. This can result in minor errors in reproduction. Possible imperfections include missing and blurred pages, poor pictures, markings and other reproduction issues beyond our control. Because this work is culturally important, we have made it available as part of our commitment to protecting, preserving, and promoting the world's literature.

GUIDE TO FOLD-OUTS MAPS and OVERSIZED IMAGES

The book you are reading was digitized from microfilm captured over the past thirty to forty years. Years after the creation of the original microfilm, the book was converted to digital files and made available in an online database.

In an online database, page images do not need to conform to the size restrictions found in a printed book. When converting these images back into a printed bound book, the page sizes are standardized in ways that maintain the detail of the original. For large images, such as fold-out maps, the original page image is split into two or more pages

Guidelines used to determine how to split the page image follows:

• Some images are split vertically; large images require vertical and horizontal splits.
• For horizontal splits, the content is split left to right.
• For vertical splits, the content is split from top to bottom.
• For both vertical and horizontal splits, the image is processed from top left to bottom right.

Renu

Autobiography

— OF —

Jesse H. Pomeroy,

Written by him while imprisoned in the Suffolk County Jail and
under sentence of death for the murder of H. H. Millen.

Together with a sketch of his trial, the several crimes with which
he is charged, and an account of his recent
attempt to break Jail.

"Human beings seem so many departures, more or less gross, from the line of beauty. To one
success is nature's evident aim at perfection there are a thousand failures, and when the deviation from
the type becomes extreme, we call it monstrous. What shall we do with it?"

BOSTON:

Published by J. A. Cummings & Co.,

248 Washington Street.

AUTOBIOGRAPHY
OF
JESSE H. POMEROY,
WRITTEN BY HIMSELF.

[Portrait of Pomeroy from a recent photograph.]

The following is the full text of the "Life of Jesse Harding Pomeroy," written by himself during his imprisonment in the Suffolk County jail, and originally printed in the BOSTON SUNDAY TIMES. The story is printed from the manuscript of the condemned boy, without changes except to correct spelling.

EARLY RECOLLECTIONS.

I was born on the 29th day of November, 1859, of American parents, one of them a native of Maine, the other of Massachusetts. The place of my birth was Charlestown. Of my early years,—how they were spent—I have no recollection until after my seventh or eighth birthday. From that time to this I have a pretty distinct recollection of all that has occurred to me. When I was about six years old I was sent to the public primary school on Bunker Hill street. My teacher, during the time I stayed there, was a Miss (Mrs.?) Yeafon; she was a real good teacher, though a little too free with the "rattan" to suit me. My brother went to the same school and teacher

that I did. I did not like school very much, so used to run away, or, as boys call it, "Hook Jack," every time that I could. My father at this time worked at the Navy Yard, and on Wednesday or Saturday afternoons I used to go there with him, and see him work, or have some fun. His work was to pump the water from the dry dock when it needed it, also to take care of the engine, etc. My work used to be to set down in a corner and whittle a piece of wood, but mostly to play with some other boys that came in there, certainly not very hard work.

BOATING ON THE SLY.

During this time our family lived on Lexington street, No. 78. It was very near the bank of the Mystic River, and some time us boys used to get a boat—for there was a boat house near us—and go on the river of an afternoon, and have a good time, though Charlie (my brother) and I had to do it on the sly, so that mother could not see us, for she forbid us going on the water without her consent unless father went with us. Of course, Charles and I complied with her request. My brother Charles is twenty months older than I am. He was born in 1858, in March. He and I are the only children of our parents.

I LIKE CHARLIE,

he is a good-natured boy, full of fun at that time, but now he has settled down as becomes him, owns a paper route, and is trying to cultivate a moustache with considerable success. He is very fond of girls. We used to get along pretty well together, had our fights and rows as well as others did; but, on the whole, we got on very well. We used to go fishing sometimes, play ball a good deal, and were together most all the time; went to the same school, had the same teacher. We went to the primary school for about two years, then were promoted to the Winthrop Grammar School; that was about 1868 or '69; went continuously to it until July, 1872. During my stay there I left off playing truant, or, at least, did not practice it so much, and in my studies I was fair. My conduct while there was

SOMETIMES GOOD, SOMETIMES BAD,

so it was a mixture of good and bad. At that time, '68 or '69, my father had left the Navy Yard, and was working in Boston driving a horse and wagon for Mr. Hayden. We had also at this time moved from Lexington street to Bunker Hill street, number 78; it was nearer to school, and better in all respects than our other house. In 1870 we moved next door, to a better house than we had ever lived in before. Charles and I joined a base ball club, and he was elected captain; he was a splendid player. I was captain one year. One day Charlie and I went fishing down on Chelsea bridge, we went on to the first pier of the left hand side, going towards Chelsea. We had caught a few fish, and Charles was just going to throw the line out again, but as he did so, the hook struck and caught my face, nearly going into my left eye; it buried itself deep right near the bone under it. We went to Dr. Bickford and he took it (the hook) out.

A CURIOUS FACT.

Now, the reason that I mention that incident is this:—that though the pain was great and hurt very much, I did not show any feeling at all, either when it was in there or when the doctor was taking it out; and now what strikes me as curious at this time, is that it might furnish a clue as to why I do not show any feeling now in regard to this case. Though I did not at this time show any feeling, it was no sign I had none, and now if I do not show any in regard to these cases, it is not to be supposed that I have none. But with regard to my feelings I will consider that by-and-by. About this time (1870) I had contracted

A GREAT LOVE OF READING.

I used to read some novels, but mostly good, solid books, and now while I have been in here, I can truly say that I have read a great deal that,—if it is not now,—will be to my advantage in the future, and though I do not feel any hardness against the ones who put me here, I do think that they were rather hasty in their decision against me. One day I went to school bent on having some fun. I met one of my chums named Atwood there, and as it was near the 17th of June, I had some fire crackers with me. Well, I proposed to Atwood that we should have some fun by firing them off; he

agreed with me that I was to fire mine first, he afterwards. Well, in school that afternoon, at about half-past three I fired mine off. You ought to have been there to see how astonished the boys and teacher looked. I guess they thought the building was falling down for they looked frightened enough. It was very laughable, but the laugh was on the other side when the teacher called me out and gave me a good licking, and after that was over made me stand up by the stove with a dumb bell in one hand and a stone on top of my head; she told me if I dropped either of them or made any noise she would give me another thrashing, and I believe she would. As you see, my fun did not turn out so well as I thought it would, and that was the last time for a long while that I tried to have any fun in school. Atwood, the mean fellow, got so scared that he did not fire his off as he said he would, so I left off being his chum; but after a while we were good friends again. But you must not think I was always bad at school; I gave my teacher trouble enough I am sure, but as a general thing I was what is commonly called a good boy. But I have forgotten to mention before that

I WENT TO SUNDAY SCHOOL

every Sunday, when I lived on Lexington street, and part of the time on Bunker Hill street. I went to the place called Mission Hall; that is the first place I ever went to; it was a very good place, I liked it very much. I went to that place about six years. They used to have splendid picnics there. The last one I went to from that place was in 1870. We (the Sunday school) went to Walden Pond, had a splendid time, stayed all day, had a good dinner, went in bathing (those who wished), rowed on the pond, had some fun in the swings, and got sick on them, and in fact thoroughly enjoyed ourselves. I have not mentioned half of the good times we had, but to wind up, when we were going to Boston on the cars a man was killed by the cars. He was walking on the track, was rather deaf, so did not hear the cars, and the consequence was that the engine hit him, and when the train was stopped the men of the engine picked him up dead. Poor man! to be cut off so suddenly, almost without warning, it was too bad. I know it made me feel bad the rest of the night, and I could not help thinking of it for a long time after; the rest of our company felt very bad, for some of them cried, particularly the girls; but then as they are the weaker sex I suppose that was all right; but we arrived in Boston without further accident. As I have stated, I went to the Mission Hall for some time, then I left there and went to Mr. Barnard's church on Edgeworth street.

HE IS QUITE A GOOD MAN.

I was in his class. One day he took the whole Sunday school up to his house in Newton. We went on the cars, stopped at Waltham, and went into the watch factory, and saw the men making parts of the watches; it was very nice. Then we took the horse cars and rode to Newton to his place; he took us to the woods, and we gathered leaves (it was autumn) and nuts,

Charlie and I, and a lot of the boys, had a game of ball and croquet, in which we were beaten badly. Then we took refreshments, went and played again; but gave it up after we had broken the set of croquet most to pieces. I couldn't begin to tell you half of the good time we had. Sufficient to say we had a jolly time, and got home all right, very tired and sleepy, and covered with dust. Do you remember, mother, the time you had to get the dust off of us? I do, for father said, "Give them a good thrashing, that will make it come off." I am glad to say that his suggestion was not acted upon. In the summer of 1871 I was taken

SICK WITH THE PNEUMONIA.

had it very bad; am told I was crazy for nearly a week, but I got over it. After that mother thought I needed a change of air, (I thought so the most of any, and so did Charles), so mother packed us off, bag and baggage, to Maine; or more properly Bath and Georgetown. Charles and I started at six o'clock at night, on board the steamer Star of the East, for Bath. It was a very good steamer, easy-going as could be; but after we had passed out of Boston Harbor, a good many of the passengers had to pay tribute to Neptune, and among them Charlie. As for me—well I had better not be too boastful. We made a desperate grab for the side of the boat every time it lurched, but something was bound to go, and I thought my whole insides was to, but by shutting our mouths as often as we could, we managed to keep them, and have found them serviceable ever since. I went to bed about eleven or twelve at night; Charles was bound to stay up, and he did. When I woke up it was three in the morning, and the steamer was just going to the Bath wharf. We had to hurry and get out; we got our baggage, then we stopped at the dining room near the railroad and had some oysters, and something else which I have forgotten. Then we started to find our aunt's house, and after a great deal of searching we found it. Her little boy, who first saw us from the window, cried out: "Mother, here comes some robbers."

EXPERIENCES IN MAINE.

Aunt was very glad to see us. We stayed there a day or two, at the same time hunting up the Cook family; we found them, too. After visiting the principal places in Bath, we started in the steamer for Georgetown On our way to that place our steamer was overtaken by a squall, and it did blow awfully. It was as much as we could do to keep our footing and prevent ourselves from being blown overboard. We arrived safe, however, at Briggsville, and hired a boy to row us over to Uncle McFadden's house. They were real glad to see us, and we them.

UNCLE MC FADDEN

was a real nice old gentleman, and though upwards of 70 years, he manages his own farm, and is as spry as if he were only 50. His wife was a nice lady. I remember her principally because she was just like mother, tucked us in bed all so snug as could be, and made splendid pies and doughnuts. We stayed there some time, visiting every part of the large farm, and every place we could about there. Then we went to Harman's Harbor and saw Aunt Nancy, and a lot of other aunts. They were all old maids. We stayed at this place for a week or more, but from there visited Five Island Harbor and the Mills. At Alexander's I was taken sick, but grandmother took care of me, so I came out all right. Next we went to Uncle Robert's and had a good time. Then from there we went to Harman's Harbor, then to Alexander's again, then back to Uncle McFadden's, then took the steamer for Bath; stayed at Ivan's till the steamer for Hallowell was ready, then we went to Hallowells, and went to Uncle Palmer's. They had a lot of nice hens there, and Charles and I took care of them; while we were there we went down to the big mill where uncle was working. At that place I nearly cut my left thumb off with an axe that Uncle had told me not to play with, but I didn't mind him, and by not doing so I received the reward that naughty boys always get. We staid at Hallowell for some time; we saw Uncle Robert there (we had two of them.) He was very nice. Our vacation being almost up we were forced to go and get ready to go home. We took the steamer for Bath and then for Boston. We arrived there safe and sound, having had the happiest time of our life—pity the school committee couldn't give us a longer vacation. The folks we visited were very kind to us, and I am sure that we enjoyed our visit exceedingly well. At Harman's Harbor

WE PLAYED BALL,

and with the ladies croquet. The boys down that way play ball different from the way that we do. It was very funny to us at first, for I always supposed that ball was played just the same everywhere. But we learned them how we play it at home. I wonder if they have forgotten how we do, and if they play just as they used to? Charles and I liked to play ball, and the Dr. said that was the reason that I had the sickness. I have not had a chance hardly to play for most three years. I have brought this down to the first of August, 1871. Of course I have not mentioned everything that occurred to me during 1859 till 1871, but only just the most important occurrences. So you will only take this as the first part of my life, for after that time my troubles came. In October I think

THE GRAND DUKE ALEXIS

visited this country. He came to Charlestown to visit the Navy Yard. I went into it at noon time determined to get a look at him. The Duke arrived at 2 or 3 in the afternoon, and just as he was coming in a salute of 21 guns was fired in his honor. I remember I stood just by the rope walk, and got a good look at him. He is about six feet in height, always walks with his hands in his pockets, and has red whiskers. The Commandant of the Navy Yard walked beside him, and he put me in mind of a stuffed turkey cock, he put on so many airs, and his big sword was clanking and nearly tripped him up as he walked. Altogether he was a ludicrous object. In the July of 1871 I was promoted from the class of Miss

Clark to one next higher; this was in school. On the 29th day of November I passed my twelfth birthday. I was glad, you may well suppose. Charlie woke me up by pulling my ears. I didn't like that. Well, everything continued about the same at home; I went to school and so did Charlie.

REMOVAL TO SOUTH BOSTON.

At about the first day of August we moved to South Boston. I, of course, had to change schools. So at the beginning of the school term in South Boston I applied for admission at the Bigelow School, corner of E and Fourth streets. I was admitted. This was about the 2d or 3d of September, 1872. After I had been at the school about a week or so, a police officer (whose name I afterwards ascertained—at the time of my arrest—was Mr. Bragdon,) and a little boy came into the school, and he looked at all of us, and said to the officer, "The boy isn't here." That little boy's name I afterwards found out was Joseph Kennedy. His object in coming there was to see if he could identify the boy who had assaulted him. He visited all the schools of South Boston, and you will take notice of what he said, "The boy isn't here." On the 21st day of this same month (September) I was walking up Broadway toward home. I stopped a moment and looked, out of mere curiosity, into the Police Station, No. 6.

HIS FIRST ARREST.

I then walked along, when just as I got up to C street, this officer that came into the school that day, came out of the police station accompanied by this boy, and took me by the arm and said he wanted to see me at the station. I told him I had done nothing, and commenced to cry, I was so frightened. He took me to the station, and those boys that had been so maltreated by another came and said that I was the boy that did it to them, and the only way they identified me was because I had a spot on the right eye. Well, the officers questioned me, and then I was locked up in a cell, not allowed to see my parents or friends. Here that night I was kept in torture, I could almost say, by the questioning and flinging in my face all about this case. I could not give an iota of the way I was treated by the men and officers of that station. They used nasty language to me, called me all sorts of names, and I venture to state that never was a boy of my age placed before in such a condition. All this time, bear in mind, I had denied my guilt; in fact, I did not have hardly an idea of what I was arrested for. My feelings I will describe by-and-by. What wonder is it that, on account of this being flung in my face at every opportunity, and the officers using nasty language to me in describing the cases, that with my terror and confusion that I was in,— what wonder is it that I requested to be let alone, and not talked to so much? And because I did make that request, the officers said I was guilty; but they would not let me alone; they plied me with question upon question, but did not get me to contradict myself, or to confess to my doing those horrible crimes.

HOW HE WAS URGED TO CONFESS.

At night, about twelve o'clock, I was aroused from sleep by two persons coming to my cell and telling me to get up. One of them came in and took me on his knee and said, "Jesse, tell me how you did these things?" I told him I did not do them; then he swore he would *make* me confess. Then he went away, but in a few moments he came back again with this same man, and took me on his knee and said, "Jesse, I know you did do these things, and if you do not confess they will send you to prison for a hundred years."

WHAT WONDER IS IT THAT I CONFESSED?

I was half awake, and nearly dead with fear, and hardly knew what I was saying. I repeat, what wonder is it that I told this man that I did do those things? Our conversation I do not remember, but he promised me that, if I told him I did do it, he would do all he could for me when I was tried. I told him,—for I had heard enough of the officers talk to know who, and what, was done to the boys. What I had not heard I denied. Now, the question naturally comes up:—Why did that man come to me at that time of night, and why did he try to frighten me by saying as he did, everything he could to do so? I think it is to be found in this fact, that he knew, and the officers at the station knew, that my manner and my conversation did not implicate me in that crime, and therefore, they resolved to try a little stratagem, by representing to me that it would be better for me to say I did do it than to be shut up a hundred years. Anything that would be likely to frighten me they resolved to say. Now, it is not singular that I was frightened or that under their representations I confessed, is it? No, I do not think it is, and my wonder is that I did not confess long before.

HE DISCUSSES HIS CONFESSIONS.

You will please bear in mind how it was, and under what circumstances I did confess. Well, in the morning I was taken over to the Tombs in Boston, and some of those boys from Chelsea came over, and they all,—except one, and he did after being pressed,—said I was the boy who had done it to them, and the only way they knew was by my eye. This one who at first said I was not the boy, but afterwards said I was, was Tracy B. Hayden. He came into the room where I was, and the officer asked him if I was the boy who did it to them. He said, "No, it isn't," then the officer said, "Look again," and he said "No, I am sure he is not the boy," but on being asked a third time he said, "Yes that is the boy, and the only way I know it is by his eye." You will please bear this in mind—that twice he denied it, and a third time said yes. Now, I ask, if that boy knew who it was that did it to him and could identify him, if he saw him, why did he not say I was the boy, if he thought so, in the first place instead of in the third? It is not to be found in the fact that I concealed my eye, for I could not, as the officers told me to look straight at the boy, and directed the boys to my eye; it is not to be found in that, but in the fact that the boy knew I was not the one, and hesitated to say I was, but on being pressed he said I was, for perhaps the boy that did it to him did have an eye like mine, and therefore he said I was the boy; but on no other ground.

SOME CLOSE REASONING.

Now it is very singular that those boys cannot identify me except on account of my eye. Not one of them did or could tell what dress I wore or how my voice sounded—in fact, failed to notice everything that a sharp boy would, and fell back on the untenable ground of identifying me by my eye. And how, you will say, untenable? For this reason: it is utterly impossible for me to believe that these boys could be taken on the street and done as they said they were used, and not see some other points of this boy; they would be most likely to see what kind of clothes this boy wore, if he had a black, white or blue suit on, and in fact all about his personal appearance. And again, their position of identifying me solely on the ground of my eye is untenable for the reason that there are other boys with eyes like mine, and therefore if two persons of an eye like mine were to be arrested for doing it to them, ten to one they both would be discharged on the ground that having an eye alike is no sign of their doing as they are charged; and the boys would hesitate to say which one did it to them.

DO YOU SEE MY POINT?

But I have before considered the reasons why I do not think I did those things, and when the place comes for to insert them I will tell you. In the afternoon of that day I was taken to

MY SO CALLED TRIAL,

the complaints were read to me, and I understood them about as much as I would Greek or Latin. I said I did do these things, but as I cannot recall to my mind all that I said or was said, I will only state these facts, that no one was allowed to speak for me; I was not allowed to speak for myself; that I was convicted on the testimony of seven small boys, whose only point against me was my eye; and lastly by a Judge who either would not or (didn't know enough to) could not weigh the testimony against me; who allowed himself to judge in a partial manner. I was sent to the Reform School at Westboro during my minority. Now I do not think I had a trial. It was not justice dealt out, but rather injustice. Now I ask, is a case of such importance, not to me only, but to the people of Massachusetts, to be decided by the testimony of a few boys who are prejudiced against me, and who think I have done them an injury? It should, it ought not to be so, and a judge who occupies so high a position as he does is not fulfilling his trust when he allows himself to be influenced by other than just motives of justice and humanity.

NO, I DID NOT HAVE JUSTICE, HAVE NOT HAD IT, AND WHAT I AM THE LAW HAS MADE ME.

Well, I arrived up at the Reform School on the 24th day of September. I was immediately put to work in the chair shop, braiding chairs. It was in this place that Mrs. Clark said I had some trouble with her.

But I will consider that in my review of the testimony of the trial further along, only remarking here that I do not remember anything about what she said, and I shall also consider the snake story in my review of the testimony by-and-by.

AT THE REFORM SCHOOL.

The boys of the school up there, as soon as they found out that I had been sent there for these crimes, commenced to twit me, to throw it into my face every chance they could get; but I bore it the best I could, knowing that the less I complained of it the sooner they would leave it off. And I am sure as soon as they perceived my forced indifference, they left off, and we were ever after the best of friends. In the chair shop I did my share of the work, and some of the others', too. My work was to make a chair and a half a day; that is, I had to braid with cane one bottom of a chair and half of another. Sometimes I got through early and helped others who were backwards. At other times I was late and some one helped me. Perhaps you would like a specimen of

THE DAILY LIFE OF THE BOYS.

It is this: In summer the boys get up at five in the morning, make their beds, and then go out to wash in the wash-room. After that, if there is time, they have a little play, and then go to school and stay till half-past seven. At that time they go to breakfast, which for the boys every morning consists of bread and coffee; the breakfast lasts about half an hour, then the boys have a chance to play, and at eight or half-past the whistle is blown for them to form, so as to go to work—some to the chair shop, others the laundry, etc. Then they have a recess at half-past ten of fifteen minutes, then they go back to the shop and work till half-past eleven, at which time, after washing, they have dinner, which consists of either mush, or beans or hash, according to their respective days. Dinner lasts half an hour, then the boys have a chance to play till one, when they go to work again in their respective places. At a quarter of four they are dismissed from the shop, and at half-past four they go to school, except the boys in the large chair shop; they are dismissed at five or half-past. At half-past six supper is served, which consists always of bread and coffee. At a quarter of eight they go to bed; that is the way the boys in the main building live most every day. The exceptions are holidays, when it is varied to suit the time, and in the front part, that is the officers part, where a few boys wait on the officers, the only difference is that the boys there are allowed the some food as the officers and to play out-doors; they also have more privileges than the others; such as, for example, skating on the pond in winter or a sail with one of the officers on the pond in summer. I was in the chair shop two months, when the superintendent thought that my eyes were suffering from the work, put me in the department called the hall, that is into the department where the boys have to take care of the sleeping-rooms of the boys, and, in fact, to keep everything in good order there; also to take care of the lodge, or jail we should call it, where the worst behaved boys when they deserve it are kept.

IT HAS ALSO A DUNGEON

where the worst boys are from time to time put when they deserve it. As I said, I was transferred to the hall after being in the chair shop six or eight weeks. I commenced at the lowest part, and before I had left I had reached the highest. One day I was left in charge of the boys by the hall officer. He told me I would be held responsible for everything that happened in my department. At that time there was the two worst boys confined in their room on account of their bad behavior. They induced, when I was in another part of the building, one of the boys to let them out of their cells. Now, I had given orders that they should not go near them, but they were let out into the hall, and the result was they escaped through the chapel, which we were sweeping. Now, when I went around —I always had to every twenty minutes—I discovered their absence, and in looking out at the chapel door I found it open, so I knew they had gone. I reported the facts immediately, and the boys who had assisted in this escape were dismissed from the hall, and as one of them was the head boy, I was raised to the head command on account of my good conduct; also for my behavior in this case. That was after I had been in the hall about ten weeks. From that time till May 25, 1873, a period of about four months, I was the head one in the hall, next in fact to the officer. I have forgotten to mention before

THE REGULAR FOOD OF THE BOYS

of the main building. It is this:

Monday—Bread and coffee at morning and night; dinner, mush.

Tuesday—Hash for dinner; bread and coffee all the mornings and nights.

Wednesday — Beans. P. S. — They were splendid, you bet.

Thursday—Fish chowder.

Friday—Soup (meat.)

Saturday—Beans.

Sunday—Beans or whatever is left from the front part.

This, with bread in plenty, forms the food of the boys. On holidays of course it is different.

A GRAND ESCAPADE.

On the 5th day of May, 1873, about 99 boys of the school got away. The way it occurred was this: In the inclosed yard where the boys play is an arch that leads out into the new yard, so called by the boys. It is closed by two doors, one iron, the other by a stout wooden one about a foot in thickness. Some way or other, I have never found out, the officer left these gates unlocked, and on Monday morning the boys found it out, so as they were coming out of breakfast the larger boys made a rush for the gates and got out into the new yard and then into the fields. Of course the boys behind the foremost ones pushed out to see what all the noise meant—and they in turn were pushed by those behind; so that 99 of them succeeded in getting out, but the majority of them were captured that same day. I was in the hospital that day, and after the boys got out was glad of it, for I think that if I had been down there I would have gone, too. It was for my not going

and for my conduct in the hall and while I had been there, that on the 25th day of May, 1873, I was promoted into the highest place—the front part; also into the Honor Grade. I staid in the front part eight months; the whole of it was in the part called the kitchen, or the place where the food was prepared. In the summer of 1873

GOV. WASHBURN AND HIS COUNCIL

visited the institution, and we had a great time down stairs in getting the dinner for him and them. He had roast pig (to remind him of the salary grab), puddings of all kinds, and I don't know but what there was some invented on that occasion, and in fact there was everything that could tempt the governor to eat a hearty meal, but I guess the pig turned his stomach, for most every thing was sent back almost untouched, and oh! we had a splendid feast down stairs. But poor me, I had all the dishes to wash. I did not get through till about four o'clock. I had one comfort, however, which was, I did not have to go to school that afternoon.

WHEN CHRISTMAS CAME

I had a nice pair of boots, a scarf, a pair of mittens, and a pocket handkerchief, as presents; besides no end of pea-nuts and candy. I went to skate on the pond with the other boys; in fact, I skated around it twice, making about four miles together—altogether I had a fine time. I also in the September before went to the cattle show at the village of Westboro, and when the soldiers were at Framingham, I and some others went to see them.

WE SAW GEN. BUTLER,

who looked just as pompous as could be. Well, at last, the New Year arrives, and my time comes for me to go home. Oh! you don't know how much pleasure I anticipated from it, how I counted the days, hours, minutes, and almost seconds from the first day when I was informed of my going, till the 6th, the time I was to go. I hardly dared to eat, or in fact do anything, I was so pleased. But all things have an ending, and on the 6th day of February, 1874, I departed,— not without some regret, for my residence there had been I could say almost all pleasure, —for home, where I arrived at five or six in the evening. My friends were all glad to see me; I them, and I anticipated that I should have a season of peace, now that I was free; how that peace was broken up will be seen in the sequel. In looking back on

MY CAREER AT WESTBORO,

without intending to praise myself, I can see but few things to censure. I never was punished while there in any way, shape, or manner; a thing few of the boys can say. In my being promoted, first from the chair shop, next from the hall, then to home; it shows that I was a good behaved boy. Now, it is very singular, is it not, if I was of a cruel nature or disposition—as the other side think me,—that the officers at Westboro did not detect it, isn't it? But, enough of this supposing. I shall consider all the events from February, 1874, to December 8th, 1874, and then the review of the testimony, both at the trial and hearing, and then, last of all, will be the consideration of the points that the other side urge to show that I did those things out of a spirit of cruelty. At the time I came home I determined to so conduct myself that no one would have any chance to complain of me, for I knew that as the police thought I did these things, that they would keep watching me, hence my resolution. At this time my mother and brother kept a store on Broadway, No. 327. She sold dress making materials, while Charles kept the newspaper part; mother also did dressmaking. Charles owned a newspaper route in the city, also one in South Boston; the whole number of customers exceeded 250; I think we also sold daily and weekly papers at the store.

HE TAKES A PAPER ROUTE.

Well, I took what was called the 3 o'clock route in Boston, also the part of the 5 o'clock called the South Boston branch; number of customers, about 100; papers considerably more, for some customers took two, and I used to sell some on the way home. After I had been home about two days I set out to learn the names of the customers and the papers they took, and in fact, all I could that would facilitate my carrying the papers; and in a few days I had learned all about it, and was able to carry the papers without any help from Charles. But I will not linger over that any longer, but will hasten to get to a point that marks another era in my life. After I had been home about forty days there was great excitement in South Boston, occasioned by the mysterious disappearance of a young girl named Katie Curran.

KATIE CURRAN'S DISAPPERANCE.

The first I ever heard of it was the next night after, as I was carrying my papers to a house on Fourth street. I think it was Mr. O'Neil, who came to the door and said, "That is very strange is'nt it, about the disapperance of that girl." I had never seen the man before. I replied "what girl?" He asked me if I had not heard of the disappearance of Katie Curran. I told him no, and asked him what it was. Then he told me that a girl had been missing from South Boston since yesterday morning, and that it was supposed she had been kidnapped. That was all he said, and that was the first I knew of it. And you will recollect that in a few days it came out that the girl had started from her house to go to buy some things at Tobin's, where she was last seen, and that a little boy said he had seen a carriage drive up the street, and a man take and put Katie in. She was crying, and it was generally thought that her father had sent her to a convent or some place; I have forgotten what was then said. You will please to bear those facts in mind, as I shall refer to them again, as they formed a particular part of my confession. A week or sometime after the girl had disappeared, a reward of $500 was offered for any information about her. As it did not concern me any, I never thought about the thing, I believe, till after a body was found in the cellar

of our store. But I am going ahead too fast. I continued at my daily work of carrying papers, as usual, and nothing worthy of record happened till the 22d day of April. On that day

A SMALL BOY WAS MURDERED

on the South Boston marsh. Somehow—I have never been able to find a reason unless it be mere suspicion—suspicion fell on me, and at ten o'clock that same night, just as I was going to bed, two gentlemen came to see me. I came down stairs, and they took me into the parlor alone, and told me that they wanted to know where I had been during the day, and I told them this: "I got up at 6 in the morning, ate my breakfast, and then went over to the store, swept it out, and at half-past seven I went to Boston to the New England News Company and got my weekly papers, and got home about twenty minutes of nine, went directly to the store and staid there till half-past eleven, dusting out and fixing the window up. My mother and her two girls were there. At that time it was time to go to Boston, (11½ o'clock) so I got my strap and went to the house and just as I got there, (in the entry) I met Mrs. Kennison coming down so as to go and get her coal; then I got a little lunch, and at about fifteen minutes of twelve I started for Boston. Just as I was going over Federal Street Bridge the bell tolled out twelve. I thought to myself, now it is so long since I went on to the Common, that I guess, instead of going to get any more dinner, I will go there, so I walked along Broadway and up Federal street, over the bridge, along Federal street to Milk, up Milk on to Washington, up Bromfield on to Tremont, along Tremont on to the Common. I noticed nothing peculiar in going along the streets, but I saw as I went along Federal that working men were building a cistern or well, right in front of that new dining room at the corner of Milk and Federal, and also that men were grading Federal street, near that also men shovelling mud from the street into carts; some of them were city carts; on Federal street all this was.

A GOOD MEMORY.

On Milk I noticed nothing except the fronts of the Post and Transcript buildings. The Post building was not finished. It looked (the front) as though it was made of iron, and it was painted a dark brown or a dull red, and just over the place where I thought the door must be, was a small projection which looked like a balcony; under it, in just the kind of letters the Globe is headed with, was the words in raised letters, "Boston Post." I think the letters are called German.

The Transcript had nothing peculiar about it, except near the top was a slab let into the wall, with the inscription on it of "Boston Transcript Building, destroyed Nov. 9th, 1872, rebuilt Feb. ——, 1874;" but then I do not consider what I noticed as anything peculiar. I noticed nothing on Washington street or Bromfield. On Tremont I noticed that men were digging up the left hand side, going towards the Common—preparatory to laying pipes. They were working towards the Scollay square; when I saw them I think they were between Winter and Bromfield streets. I also stopped and looked in at Southmayd's candy store, which is situated at the corner of Bromfield and Tremont streets. I crossed straight over to the side that the burying ground is on, and looked in and saw the grave of Franklin, which was not near the front but back a little way. It had simply the word "Franklin" on it in raised letters. Then I went along past Park Street Church. I noticed it had a number of large stone steps leading up to it, in almost the form of a cresent or a semi-circle. Then I crossed to the Common, and sat down on the stump of a tree which was covered, I should think, with zinc. What I noticed there was that the side of the fence on Tremont street had been taken away, that some of the walks were covered with tar or something that looked like it, that some of the walks were covered with boards, and that the sparrows' houses up in the trees were painted a brown color, except the windows, which were white; that the large fountain (called Brewer's) was uncovered, but had not been playing while I was there. After resting a few minutes, I started and walked down to the big elm. It was surrounded by an iron fence, and on the gate was an inscription something like this: "This tree is — years old. It was nearly destroyed by a storm." Then it gives the name of the mayor of the city when the fence was put around it, also the date of the year. The tree was very old I should think, from its appearance. It had canvas wrapped around it, and iron braces to hold the limbs up. Then I walked along till I came to the Frog Pond; the fountain was not playing when I was there, though the pond was full of water. I did not stop here; I noticed a little round house on my left hand side and walked toward that large hill near the pond; the house was painted green and there was a flag pole on the side of it; the house was surrounded by pointed pickets. I passed right over that large hill; I noticed that where the walk was it was covered with tar just like some of the paths near the Tremont street side; and went down by the parade ground. There were some boys playing ball there. Then I went right over to the Public Garden and passed through the fence. I noticed in the doorway of the hot-house a large plant. I don't know what the name of it was, but it was in a large tub, which was painted green, and had the top of it cut down. Then I passed to the bridge; just as I got there I noticed that the swans were in the pond, but I have forgotten whether or no the fountain was playing. There were a lot of children playing near the pond. I noticed just opposite the pond the statue of somebody; it was made of bronze and the man had his right hand stuck out, while his left was in the folds of his coat; then right near the bridge, looking toward Boylston street, was the statue of Washington on a horse, his right hand lifting his hat, his left holding the reins of the horse; near it were two small fountains, one was uncovered, the other closed up. I noticed on the other side of the street another park, and in it was a white statue, but I have forgotten now what it represented.

FURTHER RECOLLECTIONS OF THE DAY.

Being late, about half-past one, I started for Presho's dining room. I went up Beacon street, across the Common, and I noticed the dome of the State House was painted gold color, Tremont street, down School, where I noticed statue of Franklin in the City Hall yard, then into Washington street, down Water, into Congress, then into Presho's. It was then between a quarter of and two o'clock. Charles gave me my money to get the checks for my papers. I went to the Traveller Office, and of the boy tending there bought 39 checks for papers. Then I thought, as it was early, I would go down to the market and see if I could not see father and get him to get me some dinner. I went down there but I could not find him. As I was going through the main door, just where the clock is, I met Mr. Ira Nay. He is the one that I leave papers for at the corner of Pearl and Congress, or of Franklin and Congress, I have forgotten which. He said "Hullo, you down this way." I said "Yes." Then I went out on the corner of North Market and Commercial streets, and just as I got there, I saw two gentlemen that used to be in Longdon's flour store. They had red whiskers, and went up North Market street. Then I hurried back up to the Traveller Office. It was about half-past two. I waited till a quarter of three, and got my papers and carried them up to 10 State street to the real estate office of Kilby and some one else and Co." Then I went up to the Journal Office and met Charles. He got my other papers, and then I started about three to carry my three o'clock edition. I carried them and got back, and went to Mr. Virgin's shop on Water street. I met Charles there, and he was just going after his Heralds. I got there at about quarter of four. Father asked me why I did not come down to the market and get dinner. I told him that I thought I would not today, as I wanted to go to the Common. I folded my papers and started about quarter or half-past four for home. I got down to the corner of Dorchester avenue and Broadway just as the clock was striking five. Then I carried the rest of my papers and got up at the store at a quarter past five. I carried the rest and got through at about half-past six, my usual time. Now I did not tell these gentlemen all of this, but as I was telling you the story of my whereabouts that day I thought I might as well tell you now as any time. This gentleman, after having asked me a number of questions, said he wanted me to go down to the station so he could consult a third party. I turned to mother and said,

"DON'T FRET, MOTHER, I HAVEN'T DONE ANYTHING; SO DON'T FRET."

I think the man said I could come right back again. Mr C—— went down with me. They took me to the station and took off all my clothes except my pants, but gave me them all back again except my undershirt. They asked me where my vest was; I told them at home, and they wanted to know where my knife was, and I told them at home in my vest. Then they took my boots and asked me what made them so muddy; I told them walking so much. They kept me up till two in the morning. All this time I had not the slightest idea of what I was arrested for. In the morning a few men came to the cell door, and hollered out, "You are guilty and will be shut up for a hundred years." Then they laughed and went away. In the morning I was taken up stairs and in the presence of a great many men, Mr. Savage told me I was arrested for the murder of that boy on the marsh. I don't remember what I said then, I know I was very much scared. Then Mr. Wood and Dearborn asked me if I did not kill H. H. Millen. I told them "No." They said it would be better for me to confess. I said I had nothing to confess. That is the way they kept talking to me, first one then the other. At last I said "I might have done it." They winked at that. I was so frightened and resolved to say it so as to get rid of them. I did not know hardly what I was saying. Then they told me I was to go to see the body. I supposed they meant to go to the boy's house, and as I do not like to see a dead person, and as the men had been telling me horrible stories how it looked, they got my nerves all unstrung, but I went to the place where the body was on Washington street, Roxbury, and I went and looked at the body in between the glass cases. The man said I trembled. I don't doubt it, for I never saw such a sight before in my life. The poor little boy was laying there with his throat cut. But I need not describe his appearance. Enough to say it was awful. The man took up the boy's little cap and asked me if I had ever seen it before; I told him "No," and his story of

MY CONFESSING IS A LIE FROM BEGINNING TO END,

and he knows it; or, at least, if I did say so I have no recollection of it, and I do not believe I said I did do it. Well, they took me back to Station Six and in the afternoon took me to City Hall. During this time I had not seen any of my friends. That night Mr. Woods and another man (Dr. Green) came and wanted to talk with me, but I told them that I did not wish to as I knew perfectly well what they were about. But in a few moments this Woods came and took me out of my room and talked to me. He said he knew perfectly well that I did it, and that you (mother) believed it. Then I told him that he lied, for saying that; we had more talk of the same sort, but I have forgotten what it was. The next day (Friday) I was taken early in the morning to the 9th Police Station and got there at about nine in the morning. Then I was taken up into a cell, and in the afternoon the coroner came to see me. We had quite a talk, but as it is so long ago I have forgotten it, though among other things he said that the inquest would take place at 3 in the afternoon, and he asked me if I thought I was crazy. I told him "No!" In the afternoon the inquest came off, and I gave my testimony without any hesitancy or attempts to evade anything. It was substantially the same as written here, and a general denial of the murder or of knowing anything

about it till informed of it. Then I was taken to my cell again.

HE CRITICISES A WITNESS.

But there is one thing that I have forgotten before to tell, and it is this; that boy that said he saw me on the marsh with the little child, came down to see me to see if he could identify me. At first he said "No that is not the boy," but on being pressed he said I was. Take particular notice of this. In the morning I was taken up to court but the case was posponed ten days. My mother had procured counsel for me and at the expiration of those ten days, I, on the advice of counsel, waived examination, and was bound over to await the action of the grand jury. Now, I have given as clear and as short, without being fragmentary, a summary of my whereabouts on the 22d day of April, 1874, and what was said to me from that time to the inquest. Of course I have intentionally left out some of the talk, because it was mere talk and has nothing to do with this case. And I beg you to keep in mind that the explanation given here, in regard to my whereabouts on the 22d of April, and the conversation I had between that time and the inquest, is perfectly true in every respect. Well, I was taken back to jail after leaving the court, and during part of the time I was there I wrote out a statement, which I called my defence, as to my whereabouts on the 22d of April and the conversations, and, in fact, all events that happened to me I wrote out up to that date, and gave it to mother.

A WORD ABOUT PUBLIC PREJUDICE.

During this time my friends, what few I had, believed me innocent, but the great majority of the people thought I was guilty, but that is just the way with them; they see a person arrested on suspicion; they will not take the trouble to lay aside their prejudice, but the moment suspicion falls on any one, whether justly or unjustly, the people, led on by the press, raise such a hue and cry against this one or that one that a candid person cannot, for the life of him, tell whether the one is guilty or not. And again, as to this person who is arrested on suspicion only by the police, this is what they do: They get every fact they can from the accused, and somehow or other they twist it and turn it against the accused, and do not take the trouble to see if they cannot suspect some one else, and the facts that they get might just as well implicate his neighbor as not. The Grand Jury at the June term found a bill against me, and on the 15th of the same month I was arraigned for murder. I pleaded not guilty. During my stay in jail

I KEPT A DIARY.

I also read considerable. It would be fruitless for me to name the number of persons who, I will not say came to see me especially,—but came and stood and asked questions of me, until I got so put out with them that I resolved not to answer their questions at all, and I kept that resolution for some time. But I had to give it up, as the more close-mouthed I got the more they questioned. Things went on about the same with me. Mother came and visited

me three times a week. I had plenty of reading, any way, also a few school books, so that I
could study some when I had a mind to, which
was not very often. The officers here were very
kind to me, and minded their own business
better than I should suppose they would, having such opportunities to quiz a person. I behaved myself, and got along well enough with
the officers. I shaved once and awhile but
soon got sick of it, so left it off. The counsel
that were engaged to defend me, were Joseph
H. Cotton and Chas. Robinson, Jr., both of
Charlestown. This brings my record down to
the 18th day of July, 1874.

There was discovered on Saturday, July 18th,
a body in the cellar of a store No. 327 Broadway, supposed to be the remains of Katie Curran. As we were the last to occupy part of
that store, and as I was under arrest for a
murder,

THE POLICE ARRESTED MY MOTHER AND BROTHER

on suspicion; but why they did that, and let
the gentleman that kept the next part of the
store, and the family up stairs, go free, I never
have found out, nor why it was supposed to be
the body of Katie Curran I don't see. Of
course suspicion fell on me, simply because I
was supposed to have killed H. H. Millen.
That same night at about 8 o'clock, Mr. Savage
and Mr. Twombly came to see me, for they did
not know but what I might confess to them.
The Chief said as I came into the room, "Do
you know me?" I said yes. "Who am I?"
"Chief of Police Savage." Then he asked me
if I did not know what he had in view in coming to see him. I told him, "I suppose it is
about my case." Then he said, "The remains
of Katie Curran have been discovered in the
cellar of the store formerly occupied by your
mother. What have you to say?" I told him
that I did not think mother knew or did it.
He said, "Your mother and brother have been
arrested for supposed complicity in the crime."
"What have you to say?" I told him as before, "I did not think mother did it, or that she
knew anything about a body being in the cellar." He asked me why I thought so. I told
him that she would not do such a thing, and
if she had known the body to be there she
would have given information to the
proper parties. Then he said that I was
seen and heard to inquire, when first arrested,
about the reward offered for the discovery of
Katie Curran, thereby indicating that I knew
something about it. I declared all such reports
lies, and that the proofs thereof could not be
advanced. He also said that I had been seen
in company with the girl the day she disappeared. I said, "That statement is something
that has got to be proved." The other gentleman (Mr. James W. Twombly) said about this
time that "the girl's head had been severed
from the body," and asked me "if it looked
like mother's work?" I told him I did not believe she did it, assigning the same reason for
thinking so as before. Mr. Bradley was present at this interview. It lasted fifteen or
twenty minutes. As I was going back to my
cell, Mr. George Monroe, the night officer,
asked, "What is the matter?" I told him that

it was supposed the body of Katie Curran was
found in the cellar of our store, and that mother and Charles had been arrested. I guess he
did not quite understand me, for after he had
locked me up, he came back again and asked
again, and I told him the same.

HE RESOLVES ON A FALSE CONFESSION.

I felt bad that they were arrested, and I resolved to do all I could to get them out, so I
kept in mind that proverb, "One may as well
be hanged for stealing a sheep as for stealing a
lamb;" altering it to suit my case, "One may as
well be hanged for killing one as two, etc." So
in the morning I had resolved to say I did it,
but if I confessed one I must the other, I said
to myself; but, however, as I said, I kept in
mind that proverb, and as I knew well enough
of the facts of one case, I set to work to think
out how I could give the testimony of killing
the girl, and make it appear so. I need
not stop here to give the thoughts that
came up in my mind. Sufficient to say, that I
traced out this plan of my confession: "That
morning she came into the store and asked for
a paper, and I told her there was a store down
stairs, and I followed her and cut her throat."
The reason I said she asked for a paper is this:
At the time she disappeared it was supposed
she was last seen in Tobin's store, and Tobin
said a girl who looked like her asked for one.
The next point I considered was the date of
her disappearance, and what was done with
the body after being killed. I was getting puz-
zled on it, when luckily for my plans, Mr.
Goodwin, one of the night officers on duty,
came around to me and said: "So they
are at you today, are they?" I said "Yes, they
never let a fellow alone." Then he said in reply to my question, that the body was discovered between the water closet and the wall by
workmen who were taking down the wall, and
that the body was covered with ashes when
found; that was all. It was enough
to me, for now I could finish
my plan. But still at the same
time I resolved to make it appear that I did
not remember all the circumstances attending
the crimes, and I also knew that my counsel
would have to make the plea of insanity for
my doing it.

HE DETERMINES TO FEIGN INSANITY.

Now, as I had read something of insanity,
that is some of the things that accompany it, I
resolved not to remember all the circumstances
of the crime. I also took my cue from
Dwight's trial, where he said he felt a funny
(queer) pain in his head from side to side, and
had a very indistinct recollection of the crime.
I resolved to follow him. So this was the result: "The girl came into the store
on the morning of the 18th of
March, and asked me for a paper.
I told her there was a store down stairs, she
went down and I followed her, and as she stood
in the middle of the cellar looking towards
Broadway, I ran up behind her and putting
my left hand on her mouth, cut her throat.
After that I do not remember anything till I
was just sitting down in the water closet, when
I heard some one trying to get into the store

and went up and found it was Charles. He was just going through Mr. Mitchell's to get down stairs when I told him to come back. He did so and he asked me where I had been. I told him down to the water closet." This last incident did occur once. I propose in a little while to review the testimony at the inquest in this case, to show that the verdict was unjust, and instigated by a spirit of prejudice, and also that the evidence was not sufficient to warrant that verdict, and that the girl could not have been killed the way I said she was.

HIS CONFESSION TO SHERIFF CLARK.

I had hardly arranged these details in my mind before Sheriff Clark sent for me. I went out to the room where he was, and I sat down. He said, "I know you did these things and if you will tell me how you did it I will do all I can to get them released." I hesitated, for I did not know but he might only say that so as to get it out of me and not fulfill his promise, and that he might give the facts to the prosecution or go on the stand against me, but I hesitated no longer when he said "he would keep what was said between us in confidence, and that God forbid that he should go on the stand against me, for he was the sheriff." I said "Well, I will tell you." So I told him how the girl had come into the store, etc., just as I have repeated it in a former part of this. I gave no reason why I did it. I did not give any reason until a long while after, when I said I had to do it. * * * Then he asked me to draw him a plan of the cellar, and mark the place on it where I had killed her and where I had buried her. Here is a copy of it:

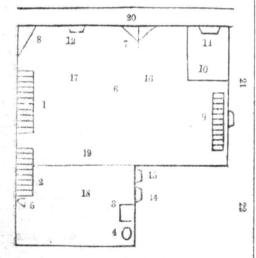

EXPLANATION OF PLAN.

1—Stairs for family up-stairs.
2—Mr. Mitchell's stairs.
3—Water closet.
4—Place where the body was put.
5—Faucet.
6—Place where the girl stood.
7 and 8—Gas meters.
10—Wood and coal bin.
11, 12, 13, 14 and 15—Windows.
16, 17 and 18—Posts.

19—Remains of an old wall.
20—Broadway.
21—Alley leading to back yard.
22—Back yard.

After drawing that, he said he was going to see himself if I was right by going over there. I told him that the plan was from memory and perfect as far as I could remember. Our interview lasted about twenty minutes. On the next day (Monday, the 20th), Mr. Savage again visited me. He said, "Jesse, I come to give you one more chance to clear your mother, if you wish to." I told him I would tell him, and so I told him just as I did Mr. Clark. He asked if mother or Charles had anything to do with it, or knew of its being there. I told him "No." I do not remember all we said. He advised me to make a clean breast of it when asked. That afternoon

UNCLE COOK

came round as usual, and as he always does, he asked if I had anything to say to Uncle Cook. I told him yes—guess I would tell him about this. Then I commenced to tell him the same as the others, when he interrupted me by asking if I would just as lief write it down. I said, "I don't want to," but he pressed me so that I said I would write it if what I wrote was to be between us, and he would not put it in the paper or give it to any one. He agreed with me, so I wrote two confessions— one headed: "At Uncle Cook's request I write this," etc.; the other, "Of my own free will," etc. The first was at Uncle Cook's request, but he did not like it, so he asked me to write one beginning, "At my own free will." I did so, and had I fully understood what that meant and what he would do with the two confessions, I never would have wrote it. But as I intend in another place to review the testimony of the trial, I will let this go till then. But let us look at

THE TESTIMONY OF THE INQUEST

and the verdict that was brought in. I propose to show that the verdict was unwarranted, on account of proper testimony; also that it was instigated by a spirit of prejudice; also that the girl could not have been killed by me the way I said she was. The testimony of the inquest was insufficient for an impartial mind to bring in a verdict.

1st—No evidence was produced to show that I had been seen with Katie Curran on the 18th or any other day of March, or any other month.

2nd—No evidence was given of blood being on my clothes.

3rd—*They produced not a particle of evidence of blood being found in that cellar.*

4th—Is'nt it a little singular that there was no evidence of a bad smell being in the cellar, except as noticed by the family up stairs? If that body was there from the 18th of March to the 18th of July, why didn't some one notice the smell as the Margerson family says there was? Is it not strange that they should be the only ones to notice it? How do the jury explain the fact of its being there four months, and remaining unnoticed by Mitchell's folks and our folks; also the fact of men working there *nine days and not noticing any smell?* They didn't explain it nor can they now.

5th—The evidence against a bad smell there is almost overwhelming. Here is some of it: First; Minnie Chapman often visited the closet and noticed no smell. (I am quoting the report of the inquest always). Second; C. McGinnis, laborer, worked there nine days and noticed no smell, neither did the other workmen. Third; T. Murphy, the boy, who worked for Kehoe, noticed no smell. The testimony as to a bad smell rests only with Mr. Nash and Mr. and Mrs. Magerson. Now, their word I would not impeach, but when so many witnesses who are familiar with the premises, and the men who worked there so long positively swear there was no smell, I am compelled to disbelieve there was any. Of course it is natural that the up-stairs family should say they smelt so-and-so, but it is mighty significant that no one else smelt it. And again if the Margerson family were so possessed of the idea that Katie Curran's body was in that cellar, why did they not mention their suspicions to the proper authorities? Also, why did they not try to find out what was decaying in the cellar? All the evidence as to bad smells were about the water closet, except as I have said, the Margersons.

6th—There was no testimony put in to show any strange conduct on my part. Do you suppose that if I killed that girl I could do it and then go about without anything looking strange about me?

But enough of what is not proved. Let us see

WHAT EVIDENCE THERE IS AGAINST ME.

Strip the case of all its glitter, and we find the evidence to consist only of—the finding the body in the cellar; not a particle of testimony as to my being seen with the girl or the girl being seen at the store; no unusual noise at the time she was killed. All this, and much more, failed to be produced, and I say the only evidence was the finding the body in the cellar. But what is that to prove? Certainly not the fact that she was killed there by me or killed anywhere by me; nor that any one connected with the house killed her. But it does prove that somebody killed her. I do not take into account my confession, for the facts have got to be proved independent of the confession, whereas it was not so, and that is one of the reasons why I say that they were influenced by prejudice; proof?

READ THE VERDICT OF THE JURY.

Here it is word for word: "That Katie Curran came to her death on or about the 18th day of March, 1874, at 327 Broadway, South Boston, by the hands of Jesse H. Pomeroy. He has confessed the crime *and all the evidence obtained corroborates his statements.* The jury also find that either before or after the commission of murder the girl's person was mutilated with a knife or some other sharp instrument." That is the verdict. Read it, ponder it, and do you not see their prejudice?

Admitting for the moment that I did that murder, the jury, independently of my confession, have got to *prove* my *guilt;* otherwise we are not governed by laws but by *men.* Read the sentence I have underscored in the jury's verdict; do you see justice? No! Injustice! Did they put in testimony showing my killing that girl? Did they offer or prove the fact of her being with me or I being with her? Did they prove my burying that girl? But enough of this, I have said all that need be on the subject and the jury by returning that verdict showed on its face that they did not judge by the facts of the case, but by prejudice. In regard to their not finding any blood, I find on looking over my notes this: That the coroner stated that Chief of Police Savage thought it unnecessary to incur the expense of the testimony of an expert to establish the fact of blood being found in the cellar on the post near the stairs; also, that Dr. Doherty examined some soot from the chimney and found blood in it.

WAS BLOOD FOUND IN THE CELLAR?

Now, the fact of the blood being found was not established. Why? Because no testimony was put in to show it, and I am sure that if blood was found on the chimney and post the Government would try to establish the same. But the *fact* itself shows that no blood was found. Why? Because the coroner when he said that did not say it under *oath;* also, the same with the other. If blood was found by Dr. Doherty, why was he not summoned or called to give his testimony as to it? Now, a few more words and I am done with this part of the case, for the purpose of showing the kind of lies that were used so freely. I include in this the testimony of Sergeant Hood of Station 9, and said testimony I pronounce false from beginning to end. He said, "I heard the conversation of officers of Station 6 and Jesse Pomeroy. He told the officers they were after that reward; he knew there was no reward for the boy, but there was for the girl. I stayed with him at Station 9 after he was brought there; could not find anything about the girl; Jesse said he did know Katie Curran. She was lost on a Wednesday. He knew the day from the advertisement of the reward. *If I thought his mother could get the reward he would answer any questions.*" Where he says "he knew there was no reward for the boy but for the girl," and that he stayed with me at Station 9, he is correct, but the rest of this testimony is his and nothing but his. Now, I propose to show that

THE GIRL COULD NOT HAVE BEEN KILLED THE WAY I SAID SHE WAS,

and also that she could not have been in the cellar four months without being discovered before she was.

1st. In my confession I stated that Mr. Mitchell's store was opened at the time I killed her. Now, if it was and he in there, and that girl went down stairs, and I ran up behind her, she would have screamed before I had cut her throat, and made some noise after I had cut it. There was no such testimony put in, so it is safe to suppose it never took place.

2d. If I had killed her in the middle of the cellar, the blood must have fallen on the boards, and have been discovered by the first person that went into the cellar. There was no testimony put in to show any blood being found, and the mere declaration of the coroner that the Chief of Police thought so and so, and his not going to the expense of getting it, etc., goes to show that he did not think there was any there.

3d. If I killed the girl the way I said, I must have got blood on my clothes, and therefore, be noticed.

THE WASHERWOMAN'S TESTIMONY.

There was no testimony of that. On the contrary, our washerwoman says in her testimony. I quote it entirely:

"Margaret Lane being sworn, says: Lives at 164 D street; washed for Mrs. Pomeroy. Did not remember whether or not she washed for her about the 18th of March; *never saw blood on the clothing*—would not *have washed them if she had;* did not know of any other person washing for Mrs. Pomeroy."

The testimony of my mother, brother and other persons is the same.

4th. If I had buried her in that place, or in fact any where in the cellar, they would have found it out before. Why? Because, first, that place where the body was found, would be the first place the officers would search in looking for the body. Second, because of the bad smell emanating from it. Third, because it would be discovered by those different parties that searched the cellar if it was there.

First, as to its being the place where, of all others, they would look for it. Well, I need not argue that with you. Your own intelligence would show that the police and others would suspect that first.

2nd, Because of the odor, which emanated from the body. To be sure, Mr. Margerson said he smelt something, but his testimony is nothing, because it is contradicted by the testimony of C. McGinnis, of C. Chapman, and the other workmen who worked there seven days, but smelt no odor.

3 d, Because it would be discovered by the different parties that searched there at different times. I quote the testimony of the inquest, showing that there was no body there at the time it was searched. John B. Margeson testified, "Searched the cellar once to find out where the odor came from," but he found nothing. Mr. Nash says, "He and Mr. Willis went and examined the cellar the night of June 24th, lifted the boards in the cellar, and dug into the ground with a stick; Mr. Willis used his umbrella; did not notice the ground loose." Now if that body was there, he ought to have found it, for McGinnis's testimony says, "removed a stone and found the body; the head and shoulders were not covered with ashes." That is to say, they were exposed. Again he says, "found the rubbers on the surface. Now came Mr. Asel B. Grigg's testimony. He says, "borrowed a lamp and examined the water closet, found the floor good, *no heap of ashes*, punched with cane, satisfied the place was solid, *heard other officers had examined it, moved several stones,* and came out satisfied the body was not there"

That is to say, he lifted the *very stones under which the body was afterward found, and he came out satisfied that the body was not there.* Need I go any further to show and prove my declaration. I will stop now. I have made this paper about this case longer than I expected it would be. I have said enough to convince you that the evidence submitted to the jury was not sufficient to warrant their verdict; also that their verdict was influenced by prejudice, as impartial men ought not to be; and also that the girl could not have been killed the way I said she was. Who killed the girl and put the remains there, and when, does not concern me now. Perhaps some other time I will write about it.

ABOUT THE DOCTORS.

As I expected, my counsel took the plea of insanity as the reason why I did those things. How it succeeded will be shown by-and-by. They sent in doctors enough, if I was not insane, to nearly make me so. Then at this time I discovered that doctors have two kinds of pumps viz.: stomach pumps and quizzing pumps. The first was not used on me; the second *was* most unmercifully. I shall refer more particularly to them in reviewing the evidence of the trial. No, I guess on second thoughts, I will tell what they and I said, reserving, however, their evidence at the trial till later. The first doctor that came to see me was Dr. C. Walker of South Boston. It was about the middle of September that he paid his first visit. At that time I did not know what he came in for; that is, what his object in coming in could be, besides knowing what I did or rather was supposed to have done to the boys. We made an agreement together. It was this, that when he asked me a question, if I answered it, to tell him the truth, the whole truth and nothing but the truth, or if I did not wish to answer his question he would not ask the reason why. I stuck to that all through our interview. I will not attempt to repeat the conversations we had. They were always on the same subject. His visits were seven, I think, in number. The last occurred on the 7th day of December, 1874. It was Monday, and the day before the one on which my trial was to take place.

After Dr. Walker's first visit came Dr. Tyler. It was about two weeks after Dr. C. Walker's first visit that he came. I liked him, for he was a nice little gentleman, always smiling and—no offence—always had a joke to crack. The story that I told Dr. Tyler was just like Dr. Walker's. Here it is; I don't know but you would like to see it: I first told him of those boys' cases, how I met the boys on the streets and went up to them and took them, just out of mere companionship, and that when I first took them I had no more idea of whipping and torturing them than I had of jumping up to the moon, but that just as I got up to the place where I did it to them, that sudden impulse or feeling came over me to do it to them; then it seemed to me I could not help doing it. After doing it to them I had conveniently forgotten what happened, and also what I do remember is very indistinct; that I did not remember but very indistinctly of doing it to them; that I did not remember their names or their appearance. They or he asked me if I remembered

TAKING A BOY NAMED BALCH

and asking him if he wanted to earn 25 cents. I told them that I remembered taking a boy under that circumstance but did not remember his name. They asked me if I remembered telling him to go into a store and ask for a string to tie the bundle which he proposed to carry, and if I remembered asking him if the Pomeroy boy was not a bad boy, and if I remembered what he said; also if I remembered taking him and, after beating him, washing him in a salt water place. To those questions I said I remembered not a particle of them. Then I was asked about the feeling in my head. [As I had been subject to head aches I told them of the pain, so in reality it was nothing but the literal truth only applied to a subject which might do our case good.] I told them that at the time of doing it and just before, a sudden pain would start near my ear (just over it), and go from one side to the other; that the feeling which accompanied it was that I must do something, which something I did not know; but just at that time that other feeling would come,

TELLING ME TO WHIP OR KILL

the boy or girl, as the case was, and that it seemed to me that I could not help doing it. That was the explanation I gave of the pain in all the cases. Whether it really helped my case any I can't say, but that I have that pain without the impulse to whip a person, I will not deny. I was, perhaps, wrong in telling that story, but at that time I had thought and been talked to so much that I really did believe I did do it; that is I believed it for a while, but all at once I said to myself that I did not do it. I will tell you what came of my saying I did not do it, in a few moments. The next Dr. that came to see me was

DR. CHOATE.

He came on the Government side of the question, and I think that he had prepared his opinion as to my doing those things before he ever saw me. However that may be, he came to see me on the 15th, I think, of October, though I am not sure of the time. I did not like him so well as I did the other two doctors; he was too stiff, that is, he seemed to be always wrapped up in starch. However, I told him the same story as I did the others; and with not the same frankness or fulness, perhaps, but I did the best I could. Just as he had been here five or ten minutes, Dr. Tyler came in, so the two sat down, and then it was as much as I could do to answer their questions. I guess they knew each other, for

THEY CONVERSED IN SOME FOREIGN LINGO

about me for a moment or so. Dr. Choate had provided himself with a report of my first trial; also of what I had said when arrested, and also of the facts relating to these cases, and if I made a single answer that did not correspond with his paper, he smiled as though he thought I was telling him lies. However, they took their leave at last, and right glad I

was, for they had kept me on the stretch for nearly an hour and a half. This was the first time he came in; it was Dr. Tyler's third or fourth. I will tell you now of my trying to say I did not do these things. One day

I GOT A NOTE FROM MOTHER.

In it she said she did not believe me guilty, and that something made her write to me. That was about the substance of the note. She asked me not to say I did it unless I did, and to say I didn't if I didn't. Well, it was not the first time that I had thought of that, to tell the truth. At that time I did really think I did do it, and that I could not help doing it, but at times something would say, "Jesse, you know you did not do these things, so why do you not stand out and try to clear yourself of it." But I hesitated, and why? Because I was afraid mother and brother would be arrested again. That, together with the idea that came that I did do it, held me back for sometime, but this note decided it. But still I was again in doubt, for

MY COUNSEL DID REALLY THINK I DID THESE

THINGS,

but I said, "perhaps not." That very day Dr. Choate again came, it was his second visit, now I had been thinking of this thing all that day most, and I don't think it is a wonder that when he asked me or said something, in which he used the words "I did do it," that I said, "No, I did not." I was thinking of something else at the time, but I did not take the trouble, or think it my duty to explain why I said so. He looked at me, and for the moment, I guess, he did think I was insane if not crazy. Then he asked me if I did not do it. I repeated it "No." Then he commenced to talk of something else. He said that Dr. Tyler had told him that I had not been so frank with him (Choate) as I had with Dr. Tyler. I told him I had been as frank and open then as I could, and the fact of his being a stranger to me, and not knowing what he came in for, ought to explain the reason why I had not been so frank and open as he wished. He appeared but half satisfied with the explanation. Then he asked me if I had heard

ABOUT THE JOYCE CHILDREN

that were killed in the woods of Lynn in 1865 or 1866; I told him I did remember it, but never heard what became of the one that killed them. He said they never found out. We talked this way for some time. Then he went away. Now, I thought to myself, as I have said I didn't do it, I must stick to it. So I wrote a note to Mr. J. H. Cotton, one of my counsel. It was something like this:

BOSTON—1874.

Sir:
I should like to see you at your earliest opportunity.   Respectfully yours,
J. H. POMEROY.

Jos. H. COTTON.

I think in that note I asked him to tell Mr. Charles Robinson, Jr., that I would like to see him too, but am not sure, so have left it out. Well, in a few days after Dr. Choate's visit, Dr. Tyler came. This was his fourth visit I think. I told him that I did not think I did it, and that this was the truth. He smiled and said: "So you said the other story was true. Which am I to believe?" He asked me if my mother did kill that girl. I told him "No gentleman would say she would." Then he asked me

ABOUT THE FEELING IN THE HEAD.

I told him I did sometimes have that feeling. He asked me about that scene in the cell. I told him that it did happen. [The scene I refer to is this: I told them that a few days after I came in here I had that feeling to do something, and I hit my hands against the wall, and after that I remembered nothing, but what I first remembered was, I was laying on my bed, and I guess I had been asleep.] He went away, and I guess he thought I was telling him lies. In a few days he came again, but I still stuck to the last story, but he would not believe it. He went away, and I never saw him again until the trial. Mr. Cotton came down, and he told me flatly that he thought I did do those things, and that by saying I did and then that I didn't, I was getting him into a devil of a mess. He said he wanted me to tell the truth regardless of anything else. I thought to myself: "My counsel believes me guilty, and if I do say I am, perhaps they can prove me insane, and then if they do, I will only be shut up a year or two; also that I *must* have a case to offer in court." So I told Mr. Cotton that I did do it and would tell the truth. He went away, stayed only a few minutes. In a few weeks after this

DR. BICKFORD

came to see me, and did not know me at first. Afterwards he said the only way he did was by my eye. He called to my mind the incident I have mentioned, also the fact of my being sick in April, 1871, of my fever. I told him I remembered those things. He said I did not look as though I could do those things. I said "looks are sometimes deceitful." He smiled and said, "that is so." He asked me why I did those things. I told him I had to. Then he asked if I had planned any of them; told him "No, I never did." He said it was very queer. I said that I thought so, too. He stayed about half an hour and then went away. About this time (November, the middle of it,) a lady came down here at the time for the purpose of seeing if she could identify me, as she thought she saw me with the Millen boy on the day he was murdered, which was April 22d, 1874, and now it was November, nearly seven months afterwards. She came for the purpose of seeing if I was the boy that she said she saw.

MRS. FOSDICK'S TESTIMONY.

I think her name was Mrs. Fosdick. You remember I showed up her testimony some time ago, and I shall refer to it again. She came right up to my cell and dropped a handkerchief as a signal to Officer Adams, who brought her here; then she went away. About this time I was informed that my trial would come off on Tuesday, the 8th day of December, 1874. I was glad of it, for I had been in jail so long that I was sick and tired of staying there. On Sunday, the 29th day of November, 1874, I arrived at

THE IMMENSE AGE OF 15 YEARS.

I was glad of it, and celebrated the astonishing event by a good square dinner; that is, with a good nice dinner that mother sent in. She sent me in a dinner Thanksgiving Day, too. She always sends one in on Sunday, some beans and bread; also just what else I would like. I have forgotten to state how I passed the 17th of June and the Fourth of July in here. I will do so now. The 17th of June was passed just the same as other days; that is, we had no new kind of food, and, in fact, there was nothing to show but that it was a day just the same as others.

ON THE FOURTH OF JULY

for dinner we had some—(by "we" I mean the prisoners)—we had some roast lamb; it was splendid; also some potatoes; and for supper we had some cheese and crackers. At about five in the evening I saw the balloon go up; it was right over Beacon street. At about seven the fireworks were let off. I only saw a few of the rockets, and them were hardly worth looking at, as the night had not set in, yet I enjoyed seeing them for they were unexpected to me. That was the way I passed the 17th of June and the 4th of July, 1874. On the 2d day of December my counsel came to see me; it was about 5 o'clock in the evening that they came. They asked me all the questions they could think of, but most every time I would give an answer

MR. COTTON WOULD SNEER

as though he did not believe what I was saying. They asked why I said I did it if I didn't. I said that I confessed to doing it so that I could get mother and brother released. Cotton snuffed at that, and looked as though he wanted to tell me that I lied. And also that sometimes I thought I did do it, and so I said I did it. They asked me why it seemed like a dream to me. I told them that what I did remember was indistinct and kind of hazy; therefore, I said it seemed like a dream to me. Mr. Robinson asked me if I recollected "taking a boy, and after torturing him, telling him to go under the stern of the boat or cabin; also if I recollected taking a knife and cutting a boy's head and then holding the knife up so that the blood could drip from it, and then laughed and did it again; also if I made the boy say the Lord's Prayer, repeating it after me, and then telling him to say bad words." To those questions I replied that "I did not remember them." Then he asked me "if I remembered taking a boy, and after whipping him, making him go into the salt water; also if I remembered setting a boy on a rock and jumping and laughing around him." I told him I did not remember any such circumstances. Then he asked me a lot more questions of the same kind, but I have forgotten them. Mr. Cotton turned to Mr. Robinson and said: "It will not do to put him on the stand. If we do, he will break down in a minute or so." I was glad to hear that I wou'd not have to go on to the stand, and I said

I COULDN'T GO THERE AND TELL HOW I DID THOSE THINGS.

I wish to say a word about my criticism of persons. I do not want it to be thought that I am disrespectful in what I say, but in order to illustrate what I think I *must* criticise, and I make this explanation of it, so that it will not be suspected that I mean to be disrespectful about the persons whom I may speak of. My counsel stayed about two hours and then went away. Mr. Cotton had told me previously that Dr. Tyler and Dr. C. Walker had pronounced me insane, and that Dr. Choate was against me, but not very bad. He also said that the trial would come off next Tuesday, the eighth of the month. I told him I would be ready. They both laughed and said: "I guess you will have to be." Mr. Cotton also told me that some of the officers of the jail were going to testify for me, but what they would say he did not tell me. On the next Monday I was surprised to have

ANOTHER VISIT FROM DR. C. WALKER,

but I was glad to see him. He made me repeat my story over again to him. He quizzed me until he was tired, and then said: "Why, Jesse, this is the same story that you told me before. It is not like the one you told Dr. Tyler." I said "I know it, I am telling you the truth, but at the time Dr. Tyler came I did think for the moment that I was innocent. I have wanted to see Mr. Tyler ever since I told him the story, and if you see him I would like you to tell him I am sorry I told him as I did." That is what I said. He said he would tell Dr. Tyler as I asked him. Then he asked me the circumstances of telling him that. So I told him the same story, which is true, that I told Dr. Tyler. Then he commenced to talk of the trial tomorrow. I asked if I would go on the stand. He said "What for?" I said "To testify." He laughed and said that "If I did the Attorney General would make me say that the moon was made of cheese, and that my mother gave me a slice of it." That made me laugh, too. He came at about three in the afternoon, and stayed till about six at night. Then he went away, but before he did he said that he would be at the trial, so would Mr. Tyler and Mr. Choate. I asked him if he believed what I had said, and he said he did. If I have not before stated the number of interviews the doctors had with me I will now: Dr. Tyler, 5; Dr. Walker, 6 or 7; Dr. Choate, 2.

HE REVIEWS HIS TRIAL.

On the morning of the 8th of December, 1874, at nine o'clock, my trial commenced. I do not propose to give the entire testimony, and if I do give any it will be limited. I do not think myself able to analyze the testimony given there, either for or against me. I am not willing too for I fear that if I attempted it I would fail, and failure is just the thing I wish to avoid. The trial lasted three days; there was about forty witnesses altogether that were examined; a great deal of testimony on both sides was put in, but the Government had the best of us, for they secured the verdict they asked for. But I wish to say this, that my counsel at the trial did all they could for me; they secured a good deal of testimony for me and secured a partial verdict.

THE VERDICT OF THE JURY

was, "Guilty of murder in the first degree, on account of the atrocity of the crime;" but the jurors asked that my sentence be commuted on account of my youth. Why? Because they did not think a boy could or would premeditate a murder like that, and also because I was pronounced insane by competent authority. The reason that we lost the case is obvious; that the jury were not convinced that at the time I did that murder, if I did it, that I was insane. Though they may have been morally convinced of it, that would not have justified their bringing in a verdict of insanity; they have got to be legally convinced of it. The Government failed, in my opinion, to prove, that if I did that murder, I planned it, or, that, in other words, it was premeditated. On the other hand the circumstances that accompany the case go to show, to my mind, that

IF I DID KILL HIM IT WAS BECAUSE I COULD NOT HELP DOING IT;

that I was insane, for no one but an insane person would do it the way it was done. No one who had his wits about him would go and take the boy from the street at that time, when he was watched, and send him into a shop to buy cake, or go on to the railroad track where so many were passing, and then go and take the boy along the marsh where his footsteps could be seen and used against him, nor would he stop another boy and, if he had murder in his heart, ask him about ducks, or in fact stop him at all. No one would do that but an insane person. Why? Because they are an insane person's acts. And, again, what makes me think the Government failed to prove premeditation is, that if I had done that murder, and had been all right in my upper story, I would have taken some pains to keep myself from being seen when I did it or was going to do it; also that if I did it, I would try and efface all traces from my person; whereas, when I was arrested there was mud on my boots and, the officers said, blood on my knife, which I do not believe, notwithstanding the testimony of the doctor at the trial.

THE TESTIMONY OF THE TRIAL ON MY SIDE

was conclusive, (I am imagining myself to have did that murder), that I was insane. Supposing all the testimony to have been true, there was shown at the trial the following facts: that when I was 3 or 5 years old I was found on the street with a carving knife in my hand and a small kitten; and that I was taking infinite delight in torturing the cat; also that at school I was unmanageable, though at times studious, and addicted to acts for which I could give no reasonable excuse; it was also shown that I took seven small boys and tortured them; making one of them go on his knees and repeat the Lord's Prayer, word for word, after me, and then making the boy swear; it was shown that I could give no motive for doing these things, but thought that I had to; it was shown that I was tried for those acts and sent up to the Reform School at Westboro. My conduct up there was sketched, and two incidents up there were given, namely: that I had killed a snake, and that the sight of the blood seemed to rouse me into a fury; also that while there I had some trouble in the chair shop, and it was shown that I determined to reform as I went out; then it was shown that on the 18th day of March I killed Katie Curran, without any motive or object, at my mother's store, No. 327 Broadway, South Boston; and on the 22d of the following month I committed the murder for which I stand convicted. "Taking all these facts into account,"

SAYS MR. ROBINSON,

(one of my counsel,) "and looking in vain for any reasonable object or motive, I think that no one but an insane person could be capable of the deeds which have been narrated." He closed by appealing to the jury to consider the responsibility they had to bear in deciding the fate of a boy who was evidently unable to govern his own propensities. His opening was a splendid speech, but did not come up to his closing. His speech was ingenuous not ingenious. Those facts that I have quoted were all proved, but still we lost the case.

HE REVIEWS HIS ALLEGED CRUELTIES.

Now I propose to give *my* opinion of each of those facts which I have quoted.

It is said that when I was 3 or 5 years old I was caught with a carving knife *carving* a cat; it makes me laugh to think of it; why, the idea is simply absurd; where was my mother, or what was she doing all this time? Why, I am afraid that if I did have a carving knife at that age I would be more likely to stick it into myself than into the cat.

At school it is said I was unmanageable, and given to committing acts for which I could give no reasonable excuse. Well, if I didn't give a reasonable one I did an *unreasonable* one; but what acts is referred to? I am sure I can recollect of none. While I do not deny the truth of those reports, I *do* so hope that those who have told them will not be kept awake nights by bad consciences.

IN REGARD TO THOSE BOYS' CASES,

I have spoken enough in a former part of this letter, so will not stop at them, only remarking that the case of the boy who was made to repeat the "Lord's Prayer," and then say bad words, or swear first, and then say the "Lord's Prayer," is one of the seven points that denote insanity, it I remember aright.

In regard to my trial, and being sent up to Westboro, and my conduct there, I have before remarked upon, but there is one point that I did not touch upon, namely, the snake story and the scene in the chair shop. In regard to the last I have no recollection, and I cannot see what it had to do with this case.

THE SNAKE STORY

as I remember it is this: One morning in autumn, as I was playing in front of the school, Mrs. Laura Clark came along, and asked me if I didn't want to kill a snake; I told her yes; we went down to her flower garden, and after a little search I found the snake and killed him or her (I don't know the sex.) Of course Mrs. Clark, in conformity with females, set up to shrieking, and said she did not see how I could kill a snake so. Now, to my knowledge I did not experience any *delight* in killing that snake, more than the satisfaction of knowing that there was one snake less in the world, and that perhaps I had saved this one the trouble (or pleasure, just as you will,) of biting some one; that I took delight in killing that snake for the above reasons, but that,—with a respect for Mrs. Clark,—I took the pleasure in it, just for seeing the blood, and that it excited me, I do deny.

In regard to the Katie Curran case, I have spoken all I need and wish about it. That

I AM INNOCENT OF THAT CRIME

I affirm, and that I confessed merely to get my mother and brother released. The reason I confessed the two crimes is that I thought as I confessed the one, I might just as well the other, and that they could but do their worst on one case as on two.

In regard to the testimony of Dr. Clement Walker and Dr. John (?) Tyler, in declaring that I was insane on the day I committed that murder, and of Dr. —— Choate, who declares I was not, I am not inclined to decide which is right. I am inclined to lean to the first two doctors,—not because I am or was the one that was interested in their decision, or that they were better able to judge of me than Dr. Choate,—but because I think that the first two have had more experience than the other, and because they have had as many as 5000 patients between them, and because they sought to judge impartially. I shall refer to Dr. Choate's testimony again in a few moments.

Now let us look at

THE TESTIMONY OFFERED BY THE GOVERNMENT

to show that I took the boy deliberately and with the intention of killing him, and that I knew perfectly well what I was about; that I reasoned thusly: If I can get the boy there (in this case the marsh) and can only kill him, if nothing happens before the tide rises the body will float away, and so all trace of my being in the crime will be lost; and, of course, who would think of looking for the boy on the marsh?

That I was seen to take the boy from the street.

That I was seen leading him away on the railroad track.

That I stopped and spoke to a boy on the marsh and asked him who was shooting there.

That I murdered the boy, and mutilated his person, and then ran away; and, therefore, am guilty of murder.

WAS ALL THIS PROVED?

Let us see from our standpoint.

That I took the boy deliberately and with the intention of killing him; that I knew perfectly well what I was about. I fail to find that any testimony was put in at the time on that point, and, therefore, as the burden of proof is on the Government. I say it was not proved. I except my *confession*, as in the Curran case, as the Goverment ought to and have got to prove it in some way, irrespective of that. In regard to the last part of the question, I shall refer to that in looking at the testimony of Dr. Choate.

That I reasoned thusly: if I can get the body onto the marsh and kill him, then when the tide rises it will carry away the body of the boy, then all traces of my doing the murder will be lost. Well, if I reasoned that way

I DESERVE TO BE FOUND OUT AND HUNG.

Why! do you suppose that if I thought that way, that I would have lifted the boy over a creek instead of throwing him in it, and, after lifting him, kill him within twelve feet of the water line? I quote

GEORGE POWERS'S TESTIMONY

on that point; he says: "I found the body within twelve feet of the water line." No, rather I would have thrown the body into the water than have it so near. And that illustrates an act of insanity, for an insane person always does just so. They carry the thing just so far, and when a man would have his wits about him at that time his is gone: he is too stupid (or *too sharp* if you wish) to know that by leaving the body there he is furnishing for the Government more testimony of his sanity than anything they could gather. Rather if I had killed that boy, and had been all right in my upper story, I would have done something else with the body, instead of leaving it so near the water, and also I would know that the boy's clothes would attract the notice of some one by their fluttering in the wind.

ABOUT HIS BEING SEEN WITH THE MILLEN BOY

That I was seen with, (or to take), the boy from the street.

The only evidence I find on that point is the testimony of Mrs. E. Fosdick and of Mrs. A. S. Brown; Mrs. Fosdick says: "At about eleven in the morning, I noticed a larger boy following H. H. Millen. I was forty or fifty feet he from him at the time; noticed the large boy as looked up to my window; he looked so strange that I put on my glasses and noticed he had a white eye." That was what she said touching me on her direct examination. But see what she said on her cross-examination: "I was forty or fifty feet from him; he seemed nervous and excited, and he was going round the corner of a house; he waited under my window while he sent the boy into buy a cake." In where? In the window? the house? or the store? She did not say. Well, now, you see her story carries on its face its own refutation. Notice she says, "he was going round a corner forty or fifty feet from her," and yet she distinguished me by my eye. How foolish for her to say so when she knows she did not nor cannot. If she did

SHE OUGHT TO HIRE OUT TO BARNUM

on account of her wonderful eye-sight. And again, if I sent the boy into the place to buy a cake, the Government would have had the one that sold the cake to the boy up to testify.

What does she mean by saying after I had gone round the corner forty or fifty feet from her, "I waited under her window? She clearly contradicts herself. But I need not try to ventilate her testimony any more; but I will ask this question: If she saw me on the 22d day of April, 1874, at the time of day, and under the circumstances she mentions, why did she not try to identify me when I was first arrested, instead of waiting seven months and then identify me, after having read of my description on the 22d day of April, 1874? which the veriest fool on the street, after having read over once could identify me by, six, ten or a dozen months after. I discredit her story entirely, and even if part of it is true, then it goes to help along the testimony tending to show that I was insane at the time that murder was committed. I refer now to the part where she said I looked excited and nervous, and my eye glowing.

MRS. BROWN'S EVIDENCE.

Mrs. Brown says: "I last saw Millen about 10.30 on the 22d of last April; * * * * subsequently saw him talking with Mrs. Jacobs and daughter; * * * * saw him a third time at the corner of Eight street." But she could not describe the person who was with him; she did not say at the corner of what other street she saw us; whether it was Dorchester or the man in the moon, I can't say. Sufficient to say, she did not. Now, from what I have said in regard to the testimony of those women, I conclude that the Government did not prove the fact of my being seen there with that boy.

AS TO HIS BEING SEEN ON THE RAILROAD
TRACK,

that I was seen leading him along on the railroad track; the only testimony offered on that point was this: Elias Ashcroft said "He saw H. H. Millen on the railroad track a few moments before ten o'clock on the morning of the 22d of April; he was accompanied by a young man; was unable to tell how he loooked or appeared; subsequently saw the Millen boy on the marsh about three or four in the afternoon —dead." Now, Mr. Ashcroft remembered how the little boy looked, but he did not, you notice, know how the one that was leading him looked. Why should he notice particularly how the little fellow looked and not how the other one did? The fact is the testimony did not go to prove that I was the one he saw. Therefore, they failed to prove that I was the one.

THE NEXT POINT.

That I stopped on the marsh and spoke to a boy there, and asked him what the men were shooting there.

The only testimony on that, is that of Robert C. Benson. He said: "I met Pomeroy and Millen near the little creek on the marsh; Pomeroy lifted Millen over it; it was about 25 yards from the boat-house; I identified him at Station 9 by a white speck on his eye." That was all that need be quoted to affect me. Now he did identify me at Station 9, and this was the way he did it: He came down with Mr. Adams and was asked if that was the boy. He said, "No, it isn't." Mr. Adams told him to look again, and he did and said, "That's the boy." At the trial he denied saying such a thing, but he knew he was lying.

DID HE MURDER THE BOY?

That I murdered that boy and am therefore guilty of murder.

I fail to see it, though they did produce evidence that tended to show that I made the tracks, because my boots fitted them(?); also that that boy had seen me and I spoke to him. It is not sufficient. They produced none to show that I led the boy from the street, that I sent him to buy cake, that I took him along the track or that I went along the wharf. They produce none to show that anyone saw me go off from the marsh, or that I got any blood on my clothes, or that anyone saw anything strange in my behavior, and in fact they produce not a particle of evidence to show what became of me during the rest of the day.

HE CONCLUDES HE IS NOT GUILTY.

I have in a former part of this letter explained where I was on that day, and taking into consideration my knowledge of where I was that day, that the government failed to prove that I premeditated that murder; that they failed to show that I thought if I killed the boy on the marsh the tide would float the body away; that they failed to prove me being seen with the boy on the street, or on the railway track, and because the government failed in this, I conclude that I am not guilty of murder. I believe I have previously said why I did not think I did any of these things. I have not given all the testimony of the trial here, but I have given enough to prove what I undertook. I do not think I can analyze all the evidence; if I could I would, but as I cannot, I refrain from tackling it now. However, I propose to call to your attention the fact that the testimony of the witnesses contradicted each other in regard to

THE LAST TIME THE BOY WAS SEEN ALIVE.

The boy's mother says she saw him last at 10.20. Mrs. S. Hunter says she saw him last at 10.30. Mrs Fosdick says she saw him going with me at 11. Elias Ashcroft says he saw him walking towards McKay's wharf at a few minutes before 10. Now the boy Benson says that I met him at about 12. Could it have taken us two hours to walk about an eighth of a mile? Why this contradicting?

Again, the Powers boy says the body was found by him at about 3 or 4, and that Officer Lyons arrived at the scene of the murder at between 3 and 4, while Lyons himself says at 5.15. You will recollect that E. & B. Harrington said they left the marsh at 1.30. Now it was then between 12 and 1 that the boy was murdered (for Benson says he saw us at 12, and he was the last). Now why did not Harrington discover the body? Powers said he discovered it by the clothes blowing. Harrington must have been very blind at that time. You may draw your own conclusions from these incidents.

MORE CONCERNING THE DOCTORS.

In regard to the testimony of the doctors: two of them declared that I was insane, while the other said I had the "Congenital Weakness and Moral Obliquity." Now, what that means I don't know, but I only guess that it means that I have a weakness to take boys and do as they say I did. If it is so I don't, then, see the difference between that and insanity, for insanity, as I understand, means desire to do it, (that is in my case.) I cannot, I do not wish to try to pass any judgment on the Doctors' testimony. I leave you to form your own.

THE CASTS OF THE BOOT TRACKS.

A few more words about the trial and I am through. You will notice that Officer Goodwin could not identify the boots of mine, although he was present when a plaster cast was made of the tracks found there, supposed to have been made by me. He said that he "found the casts to fit my boots," and although he made the casts he "could not identify the boots." Certainly it is very singular, to me at least. I have my suspicions how those tracks were made to fit my boots so nicely. Now, in regard to

UNCLE COOK'S TESTIMONY.

He said in regard to my giving the confession, this: "That Jesse made and wrote that confession of his own free will, and that it was given to me without any other condition except that it was to be kept from the newspapers." Now I never understood it that way. The understanding that we had was this: "At your request, Uncle Cook, I give you this confession; it is to be between you and I, you are not to give it to anyone, or to publish it or let it be published." He assented to that, and this is the way he kept his promise: That same afternoon he gave it to the sheriff, who, I suppose, gave it to the Government. Then he had it published in the Globe newspaper, for at the report of the trial the Globe says: "This confession was printed exclusively in the Globe a few days after it was given up." And then at the trial he went on to the stand and swore just as I have quoted. Of course you see he kept his promises not to publish or let it be published, to keep it between he and I, and that he was not to give it to anyone.

I COULD NEVER TRUST ANYONE DOWN HERE AGAIN.

I do not wish it to be thought that I am harsh or disrespectful about or to Mr. Cook. He may have understood it as he said, but I have long thought of all the circumstances attending the giving of that confession, and I cannot see how he could have misunderstood me when I gave it to him, for he said as I did, "I agree to that." I thank Mr. Cook for his kindness to me while here. The prisoners have reason to thank him; he is a good and kind man. I honor him in his old age, but nevertheless, in writing up this case, I must leave out all such as that, and come to the facts, not the fancies. It is from no hastiness that I have judged him; I have thought a great deal about this, and still I must, if I be impartial, judge him as I have. But I will give Mr. Cook the benefit of a doubt. I am loath to leave this part of the subject, for I am afraid I am not understood, but I must, but before I do I will repeat, that I feel no ill will or hardness toward Mr. Cook; on the contrary, I have much to thank him for; he is a good and kind man I cannot doubt, and I cannot forget his conduct on that occasion, but I can and do forgive him; and I give him the benefit of a doubt that he did not understand the conditions in which that confession was given.

THE MILLEN CONFESSION.

One more point and then I will leave the consideration of the evidence, and take up the consideration of the verdict. It is this, that the story of my confessing to the murder of the Millen boy, when I saw him at the undertaker's, and requested to be taken away, is false in every respect, and there was no evidence to corroborate the story. Now, this is all I have to criticise of the evidence. The conclusions which I have arrived at will, I know, not be wholly accepted, but whether they are or not I mean just what I have said in regard to them, and have said just what I meant. My reasoning perhaps is poor. If it is there is a chance for improvement.

REMEMBER YOU ARE READING A BOY'S LIFE WRITTEN BY HIMSELF,

and the conclusions he arrives at are not infallible; they are simply a boy's conclusions.

Now let us look at

THE JURY'S VERDICT.

It was "murder in the first degree on account of the atrocity of the crime." I do not see a greater amount of atrocity in it than in the case of Dwight's killing McLaughlin. To be sure, it is a very extraordinary thing for a boy of 14 to murder, not yet out of petticoats. If that is what they mean by the atrocity, then I understand them; otherwise I do not. But the jury at the same time they brought in that verdict asked that my sentence be commuted to imprisonment for life, on account of my youth. Now why did they do that? I guess it is because they did not think a boy could or would premeditate a murder so bad as this one was, and because they were morally convinced that I was insane; otherwise they would not have recommended me to the mercy of the court, or more properly speaking, to the Governor and Council.

Now I am through with the subject of the trial. You will take my conclusions for what they are worth. I did intend to tell at this time what my feelings were at the trial, but on second thought I think I will reserve it to the last. My counsel took

EXCEPTIONS TO THE TRIAL,

and of the verdict. They were argued on the second day of February, 1875. On or about the 10th, they were over ruled by the Supreme Judicial Court, and on the 20th of the same month I was sentenced to be "hung by the neck till I was dead, at such place and time as the Governor may see fit to appoint." On the 20th day of the following April my counsel had a hearing before the Governor and Council, and he asked that my sentence be commuted, because the jury asked that my sentence be commuted, and also because I was insane when I committed the murder.

THE HEARING BEFORE THE GOVERNOR AND COUNCIL.

Now, as the testimony at the hearing is not very long, I propose to show all of it here. I was not at the hearing, but I have a good and reliable report of what was said there. In reading it over I come to these conclusions.

That the remonstrants tried to prove, by presenting petitions, that the people wished me executed.

That the reason I did those things was because I took delight in it, and what made me take delight in it was the reading of "yellow covered literature."

That if my sentence was commuted, I might kill some one in the State Prison, that I might escape, and that I might be pardoned out, and therefore that my sentence ought not to be commuted.

On the other hand

THE PETITIONERS TRIED TO PROVE

That I was born or had acquired this taste for cruelty at an early age;

That the reason I did these things was that I was insane;

That the verdict of the jury was the result of a compromise, and ought to be so regarded;

That my sentence ought to be commuted for those reasons.

Now let us see if all this was proved. Take the case of the remonstrants. By petitions they sought to prove that

THE PEOPLE WISH ME EXECUTED.

Well, there was five seperate petitions presented, with 1196 names from South Boston, 302 from East Boston, 191 from Boston and 150 from Malden, 49 from Acton and 12 from South Acton, making, with those previously presented, a total of about 2300 names. You will notice the great number from South Boston. Why should there be so many from there and only 191 from Boston? It is to be found here: those two children were killed in South Boston, and therefore it is natural that they should present so many, but the fact that there is shows that they allowed themselves to be carried away by prejudice and passion against me. Does 2300 names represent a total population of 300,000 people? No, it does not, and the fact that so few (only 191 out of a population of 250,000) came from Boston proves that Boston people do not wish me executed. But who, it may be asked, are the ones that signed those petitions? I answer that they are nearly all women; women who may yet have to plead for their own sons, or their sons' sons yet. They have been universally censured for asking it, and their demand is so extraordinary that it shows that

WOMEN KNOW NOTHING OF LAW OR HUMANITY,

or at least those who petitioned didn't. No I do not believe that they proved by presenting petitions from women that people wished me executed.

That the reason I did those things was to be found in the fact of reading novels, and that I took delight in doing it.

They put in no evidence that I used to read novels except my own declaration, and, as I have before remarked, the burden of proof is on the Government, and they have got to prove it irrespective of what they say I did say. Col. Wilson, one of the remonstrants, got up and said that "his boy used to go to the same school that I did, and that I used to go to school with my pockets full of novels." Now, that story is false from beginning to end, and the boy, if he said so, knew better. I only went to school in South Boston twenty and a few days, and if I did have novels with me as he said I did, I think some one else would notice it.

Now, in regard to my doing it for

A LOVE OF CRUELTY

they advance these facts; that I was caught at the age of five sticking a cat with a knife, and that I tortured those boys; that I murdered those two children with no apparent motive, so it could be nothing but a love of cruelty. I put forward this, that I was not found on the street carving a cat; that I did not torture those boys; that I did not kill those children. But admitting for a moment that I did do those things, they would go to show that that propensity was born in me, and therefore that I was insane on that subject.

It shows in the manner those boys were taken that no one but an insane person would do such things. Why? The making of the boy pray, and then swear, and also the circumstances surrounding those boys' cases go to show that whoever did it was insane. In regard to the two children I have spoken, that I did not kill them. So, on consideration, I fail to see that the remonstrants proved that I liked novels, and that if I did these things I did it because I liked to.

It was said that

I MIGHT KILL SOME ONE AT THE STATE PRISON,

that I might be pardoned out; that I might escape, and so have opportunities to do as I have done again; and so on through the catalogue of mights. If these are the grounds on which they oppose the commutation they are very weak. With as much sense they could have said, "He might go to sleep every night, he might not work very hard." But seriously, in regard to my killing anyone there, he seems to forget that there are only men there, and that

I HAVE A PROPENSITY TO TAKE ONLY BOYS.

He seems to forget that I have not killed anyone in here, though I have been here a year and have given no trouble. Now, considering that and the other circumstances, I conclude that asking for my execution on these grounds is untenable, and none of their business to ask on such grounds; and that my sentence ought to be executed. No, I don't see it on the grounds that they urge.

Now, let us look at what my counsel tries to prove.

1st, That I was born with, or had acquired, a taste for cruelty at an early age.

IN REGARD TO INFLUENCES BEFORE BIRTH.

It is a subject that I ought not to think of or know anything of yet. In regard to acquiring a taste for cruelty at an early age I do not think it possible; if I did it was born when I was. I do not believe, though it may be true, that I was seen on the street carving a cat, or that I was of a cruel nature. For my mother's and brother's testimony at the trial says "she noticed nothing of a cruel nature in Jesse." So M. C. Chapman at the inquest on Katie Curran says "she noticed nothing peculiar in me or that I differed from other boys." So says W. Almeader, Mrs. Almeader, W. Almeader and A. Lincoln and A. Lee. The last three were my most intimate companions. The other two were the parents of Willie Almeader. Now it seems to me that if there was a cruel disposition in me they would have noticed it. (You will please bear in mind that I am supposing that I did those things.)

THE THEORY OF INSANITY AGAIN.

Second—That I was insane when I did those things.

To support that they put forward these facts: that at an early age I complained of headaches, of something the matter with my head; and the taking of those boys in that manner, and in doing this to them; setting one of them on a rock and jumping around him and laughing in a strange manner; making one of the boys go down on his hands and knees and say the Lord's Prayer; then making him say bad words; (and they say that is one of the characteristics of insanity;) and they also put in the testimony of two respectable doctors, both at the trial and hearing, who swear that in their opinion I am both mentally and morally insane, and they proved all that I have named here; if insanity was ever proved it was then, and the fact that those two doctors came to the trial and said I was insane, and that Dr. Choate says I was not, bears a great significance when we consider that though the jury refused to believe them, they came forward at the hearing and repeated what they had said at the trial, while Dr. Choate did not make his appearance.

That

THE VERDICT WAS THE RESULT OF A COMPROMISE

is also shown by the testimony of the jury themselves by bringing in that verdict, and right on the heels of it asking that the sentence be commuted. Also Judge Thomas at the hearing said he had carefully examined the evidence of the trial in the first place, and that he believed the verdict of the jury recommending him to mercy was a compromise, and ought to be so regarded. Hon. Dwight Foster said almost the same, and that the sentence ought to be commuted for those reasons. I think so, too, and if ever a more conclusive argument can be advanced than that I am innocent, I would like to see it.

MORE COMMENTS ON THE HEARING.

Now I am going to quote some of what the remonstrants said, and what the petitioners said at the hearing, and give my comments on it. Then I shall sum up the reasons why I think that if I did these things I am insane, and sum up the reasons why I *know* I am innocent of these crimes.

Col. H. Wilson, of South Boston, said that "it was not a boy of 14 years whose fate was in the balance, but one of nearly 16." To be sure I am nearly 16, but Col. Wilson must take into consideration that I was 14 when arrested for that murder, and, therefore, my capabilities and everything about me then must be considered. This speech was full of acrimony against me, and all who had spoken for me. Mr. Barnum said he wanted to know (of my mother) what had become of the bloody clothes that I wore when killing Katie Curran; called me and mother names, and said that mother knew of my doing these things; the Governor told him that he did not wish to hear him. But Mr. Barnum kept on, and ended by calling for the bloody clothes that I had hid or done something with, after killing Katie Curran. But the Governor again told him that he wished him to stop this minute. Mr. Barnum took his hat and left the place, while Mr. Robinson got up and said that the clothes I wore that day had been analyzed, and not a speck of blood was found on them, and asked if it was not a little singular.

MY AGE

was proved by the calling of Dr. T. Stevens, who attended mother when I was born. Three of my most intimate playmates testified that they never noticed any cruelty in me. Dr. Tyler testified to the same as at the trial, and in answer to Mr. Robinson, said "that Jesse ought to be carefully guarded." Dr. Walker testified as he did at the trial, and was very emphatic in his belief that "Jesse was both mentally and morally insane." Dr. F. W. Fisher thought that I was morally insane. Judge Thomas thought that I was a very dangerous person. One of the gentlemen who spoke for me, said that "the judgment of 12 men who knew something about the case is worth more than the judgment of 12,000 women who knew nothing about the case except hearsay." This is the substance of what was said for the petitioners, and I come to the conclusion that they thought me, if not insane, a person who could not govern my own propensities.

MR. PAUL WEST,

the counsel for the petitioners, laughed at the idea that I did those things because I was insane. He said the motive was to be found in my reading "cheap yellow covered literature." I have before remarked on that, also about what he says that I might kill some one at the prison. He brought those little boys forward again, and they had to repeat their story. He referred to the fact of my being sent to Westboro, and said that then there was no pretence of insanity, (for the very good reason that I did not do it to those boys). L. H. Dudley of Cambridge, argued that we needed an example for its effects on others. One of the ministers connected with the Baldwin Place Home, proceeded to give an account of two boys who had been led astray by reading dime novels, but I did not see what it had to do with my case. Mr. Robinson closed the talk. It (the hearing) lasted from 9 in the morning till 8 in the evening. There was a good deal of interest manifested in the case. These are the reasons why

I THINK THAT IF I DID THOSE THINGS I WAS INSANE,

or that I could not help doing it. Considering:

That I was found at the age of five years cutting a kitten with a knife.

That I was subject to a peculiar feeling in the head at times.

That those acts to those boys indicate a diseased mind on the subject of those acts; they were insane because no one but an insane person would do so.

Because the manner of taking the boys, and making one of them get on a stone, and having this boy jump around him, and making a queer noise like laughing.

Because of the making of a boy go on his knees and repeat the Lord's Prayer, and then swear.

Because of the sticking of a boy with a knife, and holding it up so that the blood could drop down, and laughing at the time, and then repeating it.

Because it is the blood that seems to be that which excites me, as shown by the story of the snake; also, of sticking the knife into the boy and the holding it up and letting it drop off; and that two doctors, who had each of them been to see me six times, pronounce me insane; I think, therefore, that if I did do those things I was insane.

But, notwithstanding all that, as I have said,

I DO NOT THINK I DID THOSE THINGS

for these reasons:

That I was not at the age of five seen on the street cutting a cat.

That the Government failed to prove me guilty of those first cases.

Because my confession was given through fear and under promise.

Because they did not allow me to have counsel at the trial or prepare for it.

Because the evidence was not sufficient to show that I was the boy who did those things.

Because two of those boys when they first saw me failed to identify me.

Because all the evidence came from the boys that were injured, and they were prejudiced against me.

Because no evidence was allowed to be put in on my side.

Because the judge did not weigh the evidence impartially.

Because the sentence was unjust.

And because I know that I did not do it to those boys, I conclude that I was not guilty of the acts.

That the story of my being excited when killing that snake, or it gave me satisfaction beyond that which I have mentioned, is not so.

That the Government in the case of Katie Curran failed to show or prove that she came in the store on the morning of the 18th of March, 1874.

Because

IRRESPECTIVE OF MY CONFESSION IT HAS GOT TO BE PROVED.

That they furnished no evidence that the girl was killed in that cellar, or that I buried her.

That no evidence of blood being seen or found in the cellar, was put in.

That no evidence of bad smell being found, was put in.

That there was no evidence of blood being on my clothes, (as it would be natural to suppose.)

That, because six different parties searched the cellar and found nothing, nor noticed a bad or any kind of a smell; therefore, that it is a manifest impossibility that that body should lie there four months without it being noticed.

That workmen had been there nine days before the body was discovered, and that they should not notice a bad smell, is, it seems to me, impossible.

That the verdict was not true on account of the insufficiency of evidence, and that it was influenced by prejudice.

That I know that I did not do that murder, and that I know my whereabouts on the day of the murder.

That the confession was not given on my part without reluctance.

Because the person to whom I gave the confession was not true to his word, and because

THE CONFESSION WAS MADE SIMPLY AS I WISHED TO GET MY MOTHER AND BROTHER RELEASED, NOT BECAUSE I DID THE MURDER,

and because I know that I did not do it; I say I am innocent of that crime. The Government failed to prove any premeditation on my part; they failed to prove that anyone saw me with the boy on the street; they failed to prove that I sent the boy to buy the cakes; they failed to show it was me who led the boy on the track at the time the witness said he saw him; they failed to show that if I killed the child I thought the tide would float it away.

The witnesses contradict each other in regard to the time when the boy was last seen on the street. The testimony of Mr. E. Ashcroft, who says he saw the Millen boy going with a young man about ten along the railway track toward McKay's wharf, directly contradicts that of Mrs. Millen, S. Hunter, A. S. Brown and Mrs. Fosdick, who say respectfully that they saw the boy at 10.20, 10.30, 10.30 and 11.

Some of the witnesses disagree about the time Officer Lyons arrived at the scene of the murder, they placing it at 3 or 4; he at 5.15.

SOME OF THE WITNESSES LIED,

particularly Mr. Cook and Sergeant Hood, the former about my confession, the latter about my telling him I did kill the boy, when he took me to see it at the undertaker's, and in asking to be taken away. At the inquest I gave my testimony as to my whereabouts on that day without hesitation. I know where I was that day and know that I did not kill H. H. Millen, and, therefore, I am innocent of murder. Of course you will do just as you have a

mind to about believing what I have said; but I repeat

I MEAN JUST WHAT I HAVE SAID

in regard to these cases, and have said just what I meant.

I have now said all I wish about the trial and the hearing, and the only question which comes up is, what will the Governor and the Council do in regard to my case? In regard to that I cannot say. I do not know their sentiments in regard to the case, or in regard to me, though at this time

I FEEL THAT THE GOVERNOR WILL COMMUTE MY SENTENCE.

I hope so at least. It all rests with them; if they say I must die, I am dead; if they send me to prison for life, I am dead, too,—a living death that would be. I can only hope and wait; hope for the best, wait for the decision. I expect it will be soon.

There has been a great deal said in regard to my indifference in regard to this case, particularly by the newspapers. They commit a great mistake when they say that, and, as the newspapers control public opinion, I am being considerably misjudged. It is not by a person's looks only that they are to be judged, but by their talk and actions; also according to the crime that has been committed; also by the degree of intelligence possessed by the individual. In regard to these cases I do not feel what I am charged with. I know that.

I KNOW THE CRIME THAT HAS BEEN COMMITTED, BUT I DO NOT FEEL ITS AWFULNESS;

that is what I mean. And so in regard to the other cases. I know the crime has been committed, but I do not realize that with which I am charged. Nature has given me a mind, that when anything wrong comes, or when bad news comes, I do not manifest any feeling, though I have the feeling in me. I know I am arrested for murder; I know what murder is; I know that I have been tried and convicted for the murder, but I do not realize the position I am in. My meaning may not be quite clear, but I think you will understand me. It may be that my temperament has something to do with my not showing any feeling, but I know nothing about that, so will let it be.

HIS SHREWDNESS.

The Attorney-General, in his argument at the trial before the jury, said of me, "I showed a great deal of shrewdness in the manner in which I committed that crime." I fail to see it. Was it a shrewd thing to stop that boy and ask him about ducks? or was it a shrewd thing, when I was asked about my knife, to reply, "at home in my vest pocket?" Was it shrewd to have a lot of mud on my boots at the time I was arrested? or to leave my tracks on the marsh if I did that thing? I think, Mr. Attorney-General, you made a "little" mistake when you made that statement. He (the Attorney-General) seemed to think that the murder was committed premeditatedly, with a knowledge of what I was about, and with extreme cruelty. In regard to the cruelty of the crime there can be no doubt, but as for the premeditation and the knowledge of what I was about on my part, it failed to be proved, and I have before given my comments on them. I propose to give some of my space to the consideration of these questions: 1st, How I felt when arrested in September, 1872, and in April, 1874; 2d, About my conduct at the trial; 3d, About my conduct while at this place (City Jail); 4th, and to the consideration of cruelty in me, if there is any.

AS TO HOW I FELT WHEN ARRESTED

in September, 1872, also in April, 1874, and when informed of the discovery of the supposed remains of the Curran girl were found in the cellar of our store. When first arrested I felt that a mistake had been made; of course I cried, not for the reason of my guilt, but because I was frightened at what the officers kept saying, and because I knew my mother would feel bad about this thing, and because I would like to see the boy of the age I was then who would not be frightened. I did not comprehend the charge against me. The officers behaved more like brutes than anything else. I have spoken of their conduct in another place. If I could describe how I felt I would, but I cannot, so I had better leave it alone, only remarking that I felt bad, and hardly knew what I was about.

And in regard to how I felt when arrested in April, 1874, I can only say that I did not then, nor do not now realize the position I am in. When the gentlemen came to my house that night, I thought to myself, "they only wish to know where I was so that they could make their report to Col. Shepherd." You see I thought that the men were sent from Westboro', and came at this time of night that they might see if I spent my evenings at home. Those were my thoughts till I went into the parlor, when I perceived that they were officers from Station 6. I thought of everything that I had done since coming home, but could not think of a single thing, except the trouble I had with Mitchell.

THE THOUGHT OF MURDER WAS NEVER NEAR ME.

I have given an account of that interview. I could neither make head nor tail of it, but when they said they wished me to come down to the station so they could consult a third party, I realized that something *was* the matter, and didn't know but that some one had done something of the same nature as that for which I had been sent to Westboro', and that I was thought to be the one who did it. That was my thought till the next morning, when I was informed I was arrested for the murder of that boy on the marsh yesterday afternoon. I don't know what I said, but I do know that I was considerably frightened, and hardly knew what I was about.

IT SEEMED ALL LIKE A HORRID DREAM

to me, and so it has seemed ever since. In regard to the Curran case, when I was informed of it, I felt real sorry for mother and brother that they were arrested, and I resolved to do all I could to get them released. The result I have given; I confessed, and in a week or two they were out, and I was happy. But I cannot do justice to this subject, and the sooner I leave it the better. I think that if I fully understood what I am here for I would not be as I am now. This thing never troubles me; I sleep well, have a good appetite, and, in slang words, am "hunky-dory."

ABOUT MY CONDUCT AT THE TRIAL:

the papers say I was indifferent to what was going on, and, as the papers control public opinion, so the public thought. Now, I do not care a fig for the papers or what they say. I have been questioned by this one, badgered by that, bullied by a third, sneered at by a fourth, contradicted by a fifth, until I have got so used to it. that, as I have said, I do not care a fig for the papers or what they say. That I appeared indifferent to what was going on I will not deny, but that I felt indifferent, I do deny. Looks, you know, are sometimes deceitful. I knew that my fate depended on what was said and done in the court room, and I watched, and understood as well as I could, and regretted that I was not put on the stand to contradict some of those witnesses, for contradict them I surely should if I did get on to the stand. I did not understand half that was said there, particularly by the doctors, when they commenced to talk about "apoplexy," "congenital weakness," and "moral obliquity," and "catalepsy," etc. Do you wonder that I looked, and was confused, and tried to look so? I felt the greatest interest that I could, but where there are half a dozen persons who wish to talk at once, or who wish to talk all day, I don't wonder that I looked indifferent. But I distinctly state that if I did look so I did not feel indifferent.

ABOUT MY CONDUCT AT THIS PLACE.

I think I have behaved myself; at least I have heard no complaints aginst me; of course I am not without my faults, but as a general thing I have behaved myself. The officers and I get along first rate. They say that I am a mystery, but I tell them I am a boy, nothing less nor more. As long as it shall be my misfortune to stay here I shall continue to behave to the best of my ability. When I first came here, I made an agreement with myself, that as long as I should stay here I should try and give the officers no unnecessary trouble, and I guess I have kept the agreement.

HIS DAILY JAIL LIFE.

I might as well choose this place to say something about what I do in here, and I guess I will. I get up at about six every morning, have breakfast at the same hour or a little after, then I read or study as the case may be. But I would remark that all the studying I do does not hurt me. I have dinner at half-past eleven; it consists of meat and potatoes, with what mother brings in. The diet is the same all the year round with the exception of the Fourth of July and Thanksgiving, when something different is given. Supper comes round at half-past four, and always consists of bread and coffee, the same as breakfast. In the afternoon Uncle Cook, the chaplain of the jail, comes round to each of the prisoners, and also Miss Burnham does the same, and gives them reading. They are both real nice people, and I don't know what I should do without them. Mr. Cook is over seventy years old, but is as lively as a man of fifty would be.

About

THE CONSIDERATION OF CRUELTY

in me, I propose to give both sides of the question a hearing. That which is put forward to prove my cruelty, according to my mind, is this: That at the age of three or five years, I was found on the street, torturing a kitten with a knife, and taking infinite delight in its suffering; that placed at school at an early age, the cruelty of my disposition was shown by the pleasure I experienced in tormenting children, younger than myself, by distorting my features; that, the taking of those seven boys and whipping, and sticking pins in them, and otherwise torturing them, was an act of cruelty; that I killed Katie Curran and Horace H. Millen for no other purpose than in a spirit of cruelty; that I experienced pleasure in thinking of it, as is manifested at the trial by my smiling when my counsel was reading the account of what I was sent to Westboro for.

Let us consider them in their order:

THE CAT STORY.

1st, That at the age of three years I was found cutting and stabbing a cat, with a knife, and taking infinite delight in its agony; this occurred on the street. I have two or three times remarked on this, and I need not go into a long argument to show that the thing never occurred. It is utterly preposterous for one to believe it; to think that I, at the tender age of three years, a mere infant, should be found on the street torturing a cat, I can't believe, and do not see how others can. At the age of three, I guess that if I did get a carving knife I would sooner stick it into myself than anyone else, or into anything,—I would not know any better; but even for the moment, if that story is true, it goes to show that

THE TASTE FOR BLOOD WAS BORN IN ME,

though how I can't undertake to show, but I will say that I can believe no other theory to be true except that, but I do not believe the story to be true. If it is, it goes to prove that it was born in me, not that I acquired it in after years; for where could a child of three years learn anything about cruelty except by that which was born in him?

HIS ALLEGED EARLY INHUMANITIES.

2d, That placed at school at an early age the cruelty of my disposition was shown in the pleasure I experienced in tormenting children younger than myself, by distorting my features. If that is an act of cruelty I fail to see it. Did you ever know or hear of a school boy who did not make faces at younger ones, or try to frighten them? In the school that I went to there was scarcely any boys who did not make up faces at each other, and because of that, is it to be said that those boys are of a cruel na-

ture or disposition? It would be like supposing that boys when they made a raid on their neighbors' apples trees at night were all going to be thieves when they are men. The fact that they do so is no sign that they will grow up thieves, for I am willing to say that there is scarcely a man who when a boy did not do the same thing.

THE TORTURING OF THE SEVEN BOYS.

3d, That the taking of those seven boys and whipping, sticking pins in them, and otherwise torturing them, was an act of cruelty. I admit that it is so, because inflicting cruelty is nothing but inflicting torture. But I did not do those things, and, therefore, cannot on those grounds be considered of a cruel nature or disposition. But even supposing me to have done those acts; it is the strongest grounds on which the supposition of a cruel nature in me can be based, as the acts themselves were nothing but acts of cruelty, and it follows as a natural conclusion that the person or persons who did those are cruel persons. Why I think that I did not do those things I have told sometime ago. I need not repeat the reasons here. That those acts were done by one and the same person, that the acts were cruel, and that the person who did them was a cruel person, I will not deny; but that I did those acts, and that I am a cruel person, I do deny most emphatically.

FURTHER DENIALS OF MURDER.

4th. That I killed Katie Curran and Horace H. Millen for no other motive than in a spirit of cruelty. I did not kill Horace H. Millen or Kate Curran, and even if I did, it would show that I was more insane than anything else when I did it.

HE DENIES TAKING PLEASURE IN CRUELTY.

5th, That I experience pleasure in thinking of these things, and did at the trial. I deny it. On the contrary, I never think about these things without feelings of disgust. (I can at this moment think of no other word). It gives me no pleasure. The feeling it excites is more of sorrow than anything else. If I took pleasure in thinking of it I would in talking of it, in boasting of it. It is not so. I never talk of this without I ought to or must. I never have boasted, or will, about this thing. It is nothing to boast of, but rather that which ought to be hidden away in the darkest place possible, and then only thought of in a spirit of sorrow and of remorse. If I did those things I never have thought or talked of them without the deepest feeling of shame and reproach. But as I did not do those things I do not have that feeling. Altogether, I think that the reasons I have given above do not prove that I am a cruel nature. Doubtless, I have my faults as other boys do, but that I am cruel I do not believe; never have and never shall.

PEOPLE THINK I GLORY IN THE POSITION I AM IN.

They think that I did those things, that I did it for no other reason than a love of cruelty, of inflicting suffering, and so they will continue to think until I am not held up before them so, as I am now. But I do not despair. Every cloud has a silvery lining. The time will, it has got to come, when I shall be judged aright. I feel no ill will against the public; I pray God give them eyes to see and minds to think, and then they will see the facts of my case thoroughly and clearly, and their minds can weigh the facts impartially and give its decision without prejudice. And, now that I am talking this way, I will say

A WORD ABOUT OUR JURY SYSTEM.

In the first place it is a disgrace to the country—not the trial by jury, but the way in which the jury is found. The law requires that the man shall have formed no opinion of the case, (I am speaking of murder) shall know nothing about the case and, in fact, the law asks that the jury shall be composed of twelve jackasses, and they shall be good and true. The result is this: A murder is committed, there is great excitement, the papers are full of it and men read about it. The case is to be tried by twelve of the men of the county in which the murder was committed, and as the men can't help forming an opinion of the case, or help hearing of it, as the very horses and pigs do, the result is that the twelve men who have formed their opinion, but are willing to change it if the evidence warrants it, are turned away, and their place is supplied by a set of human donkeys, who are to say whether the prisoner is to live or die. Ten to one they say he is not guilty when he is, and say he is guilty when he isn't.

IT IS A QUESTION IN MY MIND WHETHER THE JURY ARE NOT FITTER TO DIE THAN THE PRISONER.

When Alfred the Great instituted the system of trial by jury times were not as they are now. There was no railways, no telegraphs, and no newspapers, consequently he could get twelve good and true men to act impartially; but now it is impossible. If Alfred could have foreseen that such things as railroads and telegraphs were to be, doubtless he would have arranged his system so as to get men and not donkeys to serve on a jury. But to return from this digression to the subject in hand. I offer these reasons to show that I am not a cruel boy besides those that were given a few moments age: That while up at Westboro' no one noticed any cruelty in me; if they had they would have spoken to me about it, and not have let me out so soon. That my playmates noticed no disposition of cruelty in me. That my parents noticed none. That I know myself that I am not of a cruel nature.

So, therefore, for these and many other reasons, I conclude that I am not a cruel boy. But

I WILL LEAVE THE SUBJECT NOW.

I have endeavored in this paper to give the facts of the trial as they are in my mind, to point out what I think was not proved, to give a brief account of the hearing at the State House, both for and against me. I, too, have given a summary of the reasons why I think, why I know I did not do these things, and I have examined the reasons that people think I did these things for to gratify my thirst for cruelty. I have given a few reasons why I do not think I am a cruel boy. Of course, what I have said would not be accepted by the people, but I am not writing for the people; I am writing this history of my life to gratify myself and a few others. Doubtless there are a great many mistakes in what I have written, but, however, I must rely solely on the knowledge that you will correct them.

Now, I will close this history of my life; it is longer than I expected it would be. I have dwelt at great length on the events of the last three years, but the events themselves are sufficient excuse for my doing so.

I claim no literary merit for this work, on the contrary I am ashamed of myself for making so many blunders, however, you will please to recollect that this is written off hand and merely the disjointed ideas that are in my mind. Until about two weeks ago, I never had a thought that I was to write this sketch of my life. Doubless I could make it longer, but length at the expense of goodness I do not like.

Respectfully yours,
JESSE HARDING POMEROY.
Boston, the 21st day of June, 1875.

"The Autobiography of Jesse H. Pomeroy."

COMMONWEALTH OF MASSACHUSETTS, }
SUFFOLK, S.S.: }

MRS. RUTH ANN POMEROY, being duly sworn, deposes and says, that the autobiography of her son, Jesse H. Pomeroy, was placed in her hands by the said Jesse H. Pomeroy; that the manuscript is wholly in his handwriting; that the publication under the above title in the BOSTON SUNDAY TIMES is a verbatim report from said manuscript; that she believes, and has reason to believe, that the composition of said autobiography is wholly and exclusively the work of the said Jesse H., and that the same was written by him without the assistance of any person.

MRS. R. A. POMEROY.

Subscribed and sworn to before me this 24th day of July, 1875.

RUSSELL. H. CONWELL,
Justice of the Peace.

JESSE H. POMEROY.

CRIMES WITH WHICH HE IS CHARGED
AND EVIDENCE AT HIS TRIAL.

Most readers of the foregoing autobiography are doubtless more or less familiar with the history of the several crimes with which Jesse H. Pomeroy stands accused; but thinking there may be many who would like to study the case further, we propose to give a brief account of them with the most important evidence introduced at his trial and extracts from the arguments of the counsel. If Jesse H. Pomeroy is the bloodthirsty criminal portrayed by the newspapers under the title of the "Boy Fiend,"—if he is guilty of all the crimes with which he is charged,—then he is a moral monstrosity never before paralleled in history. If he is innocent, as he claims to be in the foregoing autobiography, then he is the victim of a chain of circumstantial and direct evidence the most convincing, and much stronger than is usually required for the conviction of a criminal. Whether guilty or innocent, his is the extraordinary case of modern times and well worthy the careful study of the student of human nature.

Sometime about Christmas, in 1871, a little son of Mr. Paine, of Chelsea, was enticed upon Powder Horn Hill, in that city, and after being tied to a post, was most cruelly beaten with a rope and left helpless. Similar acts were frequent during the following year. February 21, 1872, a lad named Tracy B. Hayden was stripped, tied to a post and beaten with boards and a rope, breaking the bridge of his nose, knocking out several of his teeth and inflicting other terrible injuries.

July 4th, Johnny Balch was taken to Powder Horn Hill, stripped, gagged and terribly beaten, and then carried to an inlet where his wounds were washed in salt water.

In August of the same year Harry Austin was treated in the same barbarous manner at South Boston, and a short time after George E. Pratt was induced to go on board a yacht where he was stripped and after being punctured with pins and needles was left insensible and bleeding. Charles A. Gould was taken from South Boston in September 1872 to the vicinity of the Hartford and Erie Railroad, and there stripped and tied to a telegraph pole and whipped and cut about the head with a pen-knife. Joseph W. Kennedy and Robert E. Maies were maltreated in a similar manner about the same time. For these crimes young Pomeroy was arrested as he has described, and sent to the Reform School at Westboro during his minority. In February, 1874 he was pardoned and returned to his mother's in South Boston.

On the 22d day of April following, Horace H. Millen, a little boy about four and half years of age was taken to the marsh lands near South Boston and cruelly murdered. The same evening Jesse was arrested for the crime. An indictment having been returned against him, he was committed, and on the 8th of December, 1874 his trial began in the Supreme Judicial Court at Boston.

Chief Justice Gray and Associate Justice Morton were on the bench. The Government was represented by Attorney General Train and District Attorney May, and the interests of the prisoner were guarded by the Hon. Chas. Robinson Jr. and Joseph H. Cotton, Esq., both of Charlestown.

OPENING OF THE TRIAL.

After the usual formalities of the Court the process of empanelling a jury was begun. Pomeroy looked cool and collected although he met the concentrated gaze of the crowd that filled the court room. With the exception of an occasional twitch of the muscles of the face he controlled his feelings and presented a tolerably unmoved exterior. The jury having been selected, duly sworn and qualified, the indictment was read by the clerk. It was found at the June term of the Grand Jury and set forth that on the 22d of April, 1874, Jesse Harding Pomeroy inflicted with a sharp knife certain mortal wounds upon the head, arms, neck, breast, and other parts of the person of Horace H. Millen, of which the said Millen died, and that the assault was feloniously committed and the perpetrator guilty of murder.

District Attorney May opened the case for the government, after which the first witness, Horace H. Moses, a surveyor who had made a diagram of the localities liable to be mentioned during the trial, was called.

He pointed out the position of Mrs. Pomeroy's store, the residence of the Millen boy, the line of tracks probably made by the murderer and his victim, the place where the body was found and the path pursued by the murderer on his return from the scene of the tragedy.

Chas. E. Powers, a lad of twelve years, who with his brother a deaf mute, was out on the marshes in search of clams on the day of the murder, testified to finding the body of the Millen boy, about twelve feet from the water line and close to a small creek.

Patrick Wise who was out shooting on the marshes corroborated many of the statements made by Powers and then gave a vivid description of the appearance of the dead body. He said that when he reached the scene of the occurrence blood was issuing from both eyes, the throat was cut and six stabs were found in each hand.

Obed Goodspeed who was in company with Mr. Wise merely substantiated the latter's testimony.

Officer Roswell M. Lyons testified to being brought to the scene of the murder by a deaf mute, the brother of the boy Powers.

Sergeant H. O. Goodwin of the police testified to being present when a plaster cast was made of the tracks of the supposed murderer and his victim; witness had followed the trail from the place where they jumped off McKay's wharf for about 100 feet and found that the boots taken from the feet of the dead boy and those of Jesse H. Pomeroy fitted exactly in the respective tracks; he could not identify the boots.

Dr. Ira Allen, who acted as coroner at the inquest described minutely the wounds found upon the body and identified the articles of clothing exhibited.

A medium sized pocket knife which was acknowledged by Pomeroy at the inquest as his propery was identified.

At that time it was stained with something which resembled blood though at present the marks were not so distinct as when he first saw them.

Mrs. Eleanor Fosdick testified that she lived close to the house of Mr. Millen, that on the day of the murder at about eleven o'clock she saw the Millen boy going round the corner of a house and the boy Pomeroy following him.

She described the dress of both and identified that of young Millen which was exhibited.

Under cross examination she stated that she was forty or fifty feet away but noticed the larger boy as he looked up to the window; he acted peculiar and as though he had been doing something wrong; the little boy went into a store, bought a cake, and came out and gave part of it to the large boy; the large boy looked so strange that I looked at him the second time with my glasses: he was evidently excited; I went to the jail two weeks ago to pick out Pomeroy; the little boy I never saw before the day and time described.

I looked at a large number of prisoners in their cells before coming to the right one. No one gave me any information as to what cell he was in or how he looked. When I reached his cell I knew him.

Mrs. Leonora Millen testified: Am mother of the deceased, Horace H. Millen; last saw him alive at twenty minutes past ten o'clock on the 22d of April last; I gave him a number of pennies before he went; he was four years old last January. [Witness when shown the bloody clothes of her child, which she identified, was much overcome and allowed to retire.]

Sarah Hunting testified: I live on Dorchester street; saw the Millen boy on that street on the day of the murder between ten and eleven o'clock; spoke with him and he showed me a cent; there were other children with him at the time, one of them a large lop-shouldered boy; didn't notice him particularly; do not know the prisoner and never saw him before.

Elias Ashcroft testified: Saw the Millen boy about twelve o'clock on the day his body was found; he was on the railroad going out towards McKay's wharf and a large boy was leading him; cannot describe the large boy nor do I know how he was dressed; he was either a man or a large boy.

THE MOST IMPORTANT WITNESS

was Robert C. Benson, who testified: Am fifteen years old; remember the finding of the Millen boy's body; I was on the marsh digging clams; when I was going away I met the prisoner and the Millen boy; Pomeroy asked me what the men were shooting; it was near a small creek; they were going towards the place where the body was found; Pomeroy was beating the Millen boy and when crossing a creek he carried him; never saw either boy before; saw the Pomeroy boy at the 9th Station and see him now in court; when on the marsh I noticed that he had a white right eye. I was close to the boys on the marsh; Pomeroy called me with a whistle; officer Adams was with me when I looked at Pomeroy in the 9th Station; did not fail to recognize him there.

Edward H. Harrington, who was on the marsh digging clams on the day of the murder, testified to seeing a boy running away from the place where the body was found.

Officer Thomas H. Adams testified that he arrested the defendant about ten o'clock on the night of the murder; at that time there was a long scratch on his face, starting at the mouth and running back to the left ear; it looked something like that usually made by a cat; there were other marks of violence on Pomeroy's face, all evidently new and fresh; the prisoner explained these by stating that he had cut himself while shaving.

Sergeant Charles Wood, of Station 9, testified that when brought face to face with the body of the Millen boy at Waterman's shop, Pomeroy confessed to killing him and requested to be taken away from the place.

Other unimportant witnesses were called after which District Attorney May read the testimony given by Pomeroy at the coroner's inquest held two days after the murder. It was substantially the same as given in the preceding autobiography and as related to the officers on the night of his arrest.

Rufus R. Cooke, lay chaplain of the county jail, was the next witness. A document was handed to him which he recognized as the written confession of the boy Jesse, made of his own free will and given to him with the only condition that he should keep it from the papers. The document recites the manner of killing the Millen boy with minute particulars and gives as a reason for the deed at the close "that he could not help it." With the reading of this confession the government rested the case.

OPENING FOR THE DEFENCE—MR. ROBINSON'S ARGUMENT.

Mr. Robinson then opened the defence in a very ingenious speech. He started out by virtually admitting the truth of the indictment, but held that the defendant was, at the time when the crime was committed, in that stage of life in which the law cannot decide whether a person is responsible or not. Before a child has reached the age of seven years, the law holds that it is not capable of committing any crime; between seven and fourteen is the debatable period, and no definite conclusion has as yet been reached. He then went back to the infant years of the boy and held that he had always shown peculiar tendencies towards blood and cruelty. At the age of five, he was caught in the act of torturing a cat by stabbing and cutting it. At school, he was unmanageable, al-

though at times studious, and addicted to committing acts for which he could give no reasonable excuse. In December, 1871, he took a boy up on Powder Horn Hill, Chelsea, and, after torturing him with pins and knives, sent him home. This he repeated in February, 1872, and at subsequent periods, with different boys. When the family moved to South Boston, he resumed his nefarious practices. His commission to the State Reform School, his conduct while there and his subsequent release were all briefly sketched, as well as his determination to reform when he came home. He was released in February, but on the 18th of March he killed, without any motive or object, the little girl, Katie Curran, at his mother's store at No. 327 Broadway, and on the 22d of the following month he committed the murder for which he is now on trial. Taking all these facts into account, and looking in vain for any object or reasonable motive, Mr. Robinson thought that only an insane person could be capable of doing the deeds which had been narrated. He then gave a definition of insanity, and quoted the statute referring to this class of criminals, and closed by appealing to the jury to consider the responsibility they had to bear, in deciding the fate of a lad who was evidently unable to govern his own propensities.

TESTIMONY OF JESSE'S MOTHER.

Mrs. Ruth Ann Pomeroy, the mother of the accused, was then called to the stand as the first witness for the defence. She testified that the boy, when very young, had a violent attack of sickness, which almost reduced him to a skeleton; in April, 1871, he was again sick, and, as the witness stated, was for two or three days "out of his head;" he was subject to severe headaches, pains in his eyes and dizziness; was addicted to dreaming extravagant dreams, which usually haunted him on the following day. She underwent a sharp cross-examination from the Attorney-General, but her evidence was not materially changed.

Francis J. Almeder, who lived for several years in the Pomeroy family, had noticed peculiarities in Jesse's conduct; he frequently left his playmates and sat down on the sidewalk, complaining of violent headaches, etc.

SECOND DAY OF THE TRIAL.

There was a large attendance in the Court room and the testimony of the experts both for and against the theory of insanity was very interesting, as bearing directly on a question in science which has as yet baffled the best minds in the profession. Unimportant evidence was given by Hannah F. Almeder as to Jesse's strange actions while the family lived in Charlestown, and Mrs. Lucy Ann Kelly testified that she found him one day in the yard with a small kitten in his hands which he had cut and stabbed. This was when he was about three years old.

Mr. Robinson then read the record of the Court for the trial of Juvenile offenders, where Jesse was tried and adjudged guilty of acts of cruelty to boys of his own age or younger, and for which he was sentenced to the reform school Sept. 20, 1872.

Tracy B. Hayden, a lad of ten years, John Balch about the same age, and Joseph W. Kennedy and Chas. A. Gould were all put upon the stand and testified to the cruelties inflicted upon them and identified Pomeroy with more or less certainty as the boy who punished them. In addition to being whipped and beaten Pratt was bitten and pins were stuck in his face and neck, and the lad Gould received several stabs with a knife.

Mrs. Laura Clark, a teacher in the Reform School testified that his general conduct at the school was good, though on one occasion when she reprimanded him he appeared terribly excited, and at another when she had called on him to kill a snake he had jumped upon it and mangled it in a fearful manner, showing symptoms of a terrible desire to shed blood.

William L. Miller, also teacher in the Reform School testified that his behavior was most excellent while there, so much so that he never was obliged to punish or reprimand him.

Mr. Robinson here submitted the confession made by the defendant that he killed Katie Curran. The document gave the details of murder in the cellar on Broadway So. Boston, in March, 1874, where the body was found three months after.

TESTIMONY OF THE EXPERTS.

Dr. John C. Tyler who had made a specialty of treating the insane since 1853, was then put upon the stand. He had visited the boy in his cell four or five times and conversed with him on a variety of subjects. The principal circumstance which would bear on the sanity of the prisoner, was in his opinion the extraordinariness of his acts; there was no motive, at least no ordinary motive. The violent headaches, the desire for blood and other strange proclivities, denoted by the overt acts of the accused, were clear indications of insanity. The circumstances were cumulative in their nature and bearing. No one act would be positive evidence as to the mental condition of the subject. The prisoner gave no reason for his strange conduct and wound up all his statements by the simple assertion, "I had to." Comparing this case with others in his experience he had met with parallel circumstances, though not so extensively developed or so disastrous in their consequences. The time in life when mental derangements were most likely to occur was about the time of puberty. Another circumstance which tended strongly to establish the theory of mental disorder was the utter insensibility of the accused to the consequences of his acts; the only evidence of tenderness towards any one which he had manifested being in the case of his mother and brother, whom he wished to exonerate from all complicity in his crimes. A short time before the commission of these terrible deeds he said he usually felt a pressure on his head, which started about the region of his chest and passed over or through his brain—according to medical testimony a strong symptom of epilepsy. On the cross-examination Dr. Tyler said that all the accessories to the crimes were consistent with a sane mind. His going to secluded spots, avoiding observation and espionage so far as possible, misleading his victims by giving them fictitious names and places of residence, and otherwise manifesting a desire to keep his crimes locked in his own breast, all tended to prove mental abilities of a high order rather than the contrary. A love of cruelty for the sake of cruelty might constitute a motive for acts of cruelty.

Dr. Clement A. Walker, superintendent of the Boston Lunatic Hospital, was next called. He had given the subject of insanity his attention almost exclusively for twenty-five years and during that time had treated some two thousand patients. From interviews and the evidence during the trial he had formed the opinion that at the time the murder of Horace Millen was committed its perpetrator was laboring under a mental disorder; the reasons for this belief were the extraordinary number and nature of the crimes committed, and the lack of all reasonable motive. During the examinations of the prisoner in jail, he had given every indication of insanity, and showed not a particle of pity or remorse, with one or two slight exceptions; he had no visible sign of any such thing as moral responsibility, and seemed dead to all the finer emotions possessed by sane persons; he believed from all the observations he had made that the boy was the subject of epilepsy. An insane man might be able to determine between right and wrong and still be compelled by the violence of his mental disease to adopt the wrong, although inclination might lead in just the opposite direction. He was not prepared to give a decided opinion upon the question of monomania as he never had met a case of clear insanity on one particular point where the mind was completely sound on all others. He firmly believed that at the time the deed was committed its perpetrator was wholly irresponsible on account of mental aberration. He believed from his observations that the mind of the prisoner was diseased and that if the same process of increase in the disorder continued a time would come when his mental powers would disappear altogether. An act of atrocity without a motive, he considered evidence of an unsound mind, but the mere evidence during the trial was not sufficient to establish insanity. The fact that the boy ran away after committing the act proves that he was conscious that he had done wrong.

EXPERT TESTIMONY FOR THE GOVERNMENT.

Dr. Geo. T. Choate an expert in insanity from New York, who had been Superintendent of the State Asylum at Taunton for seventeen years and who since his removal to New York had treated a large number of patients, among them Horace Greeley, was put upon the stand by the counsel for the Commonwealth. From the evidence given at the trial he was not decided as to the sanity or insanity of the accused. He had two interviews with Pomeroy in the month of October; he questioned him closely as to his mental and moral faculties and found him apt to learn and to retain knowledge; he admitted that he done wrong and spoke at some length on the legal consequences of his barbarities; he knew the authorities would not hang him, as he was too young and expected that they would either send him to the State Prison or to a lunatic asylum. In the second interview he denied the greater portion of his first confession and said that his former course was dictated by a desire to shield his mother and brother and made other contradictory assertions which seemed to me the result of education on the subject. From these and other facts which he had gleaned he was firmly convinced that the acts were not the result of insanity, at least of the ordinary kind. He was unwilling to accept the theory of irresistible impulse unless it was fortified by more palpable signs and evidences of mental disease. He was of the opinion that on the day of the murder of the Millen boy, Jesse Pomeroy's mind was free from any disorder, though he believed the boy's mind differed from the minds of others in its proneness to a certain kind of evil and a lack of energy to resist the impulse, but it was a difference in degree rather than kind. He was cross examined at some length as to previous statements made in writing which were somewhat contradictory to his testimony, but no material invalidation was effected.

This closed the testimony for both sides and the Court adjourned at a few minutes before six to the next day at nine o'clock.

THIRD DAY.

After able arguments, by the senior counsel for the defence and by the Attorney General for the government, Chief Justice Gray delivered the charge to the jury. He stated that the only duty they had to perform was to decide on the weight of the evidence put in, without regard to the responsibilities of the Commonwealth, the Legislative or Judicial departments or the policy of the government. The first point to be decided was whether Jesse H. Pomeroy killed Horace H. Millen; next, what degree of murder it was. If the accused was a responsible being at the time the murder was committed it was murder of the first degree. If a boy was fourteen years of age or over, and of the ordinary capacities and of sound mind, he was according to law, responsible for his acts. On the value of the expert testimony he descanted at considerable length. The counsel for the defence had claimed that their client knew that his acts were wrong, but that he was drawn on by an irresistible impulse and was actually forced into their commission. This they claimed to be insanity. Dr. Tyler and Dr. Walker testified that the boy was insane, while Dr. Choate was of the opinion, and so deposed, that he was posessed of all his mental faculties and in a sound condition. It was for the jury to determine how far that expert testimony should go in deciding the question of insanity. He then gave the usual instructions as to the nature and consequences of the several verdicts liable to be rendered, and committed the case to them at 5 P. M.

THE JURY ASK FOR INFORMATION.

At 8:20, after an absence of two hours and a half, the jury asked for information on the following points: First—if the prisoner took the Millen boy down to the marsh with the intention of inflicting tortures upon him such as had been inflicted upon the other boys and after getting him there he concluded at the last moment to kill him, would such an act be premeditated malice aforethought, within the meaning of the law? Second—does a homicide committed under circumstances of extreme atrocity, unaccompanied by premeditation constitute murder in the first degree?

On the first question, after some consultation the Court decided that it did not require any specified time to constitute premeditation, and the malice aforethought would exist if the resolution to kill was formed before the act was committed. Several familiar illustrations were given as examples of premeditated action which was almost momentary. The second question was answered by the statute which states that a homicide committed under circumstances of extreme atrocity, or with premeditated malice aforethought constitutes murder in the first degree. With this information the jury again went into session.

THE VERDICT.

At 10:10 P. M., after four hours and twenty minutes' deliberation, the jury returned and rendered a verdict of murder in the first degree. Pomeroy was slightly affected, although his mother who sat a few benches away was almost insensible.

The Chief Justice announced that he had received two documents signed by every member of the jury; the first gave the ground upon which the verdict was rendered, viz: on account of the atrocity of the crime; and the second asked that the usual penalty for murder in the first degree be commuted to imprisonment for life. The latter he said he would submit to the Governor and Council.

HEARING BEFORE THE GOVERNOR AND COUNCIL.

On the 20th of February 1875, after the over-ruling by the Supreme Judicial Court of exceptions taken by his counsel at the trial, Pomeroy was sentenced to be hung. In April following a hearing was had before the Governor and council on a petition for the commutation of his sentence to imprisonment for life. Strong arguments were submitted both for and against, and a deep interest was manifested in the case, the Green Room at the State House being crowded with interested spectators, a large number of whom were women. Considerable comment was elicited by the presenta-

tion of a petition that the law be carried into execution, bearing the signatures of seventy-seven ladies, all of more or less distinction and mostly residents of the wealthy section of Boston. Hon. Dwight Foster, Judge Thomas, John A. Nowell, the Rev. W. H. H. Murray and several others spoke in favor of commutation, and Paul West, Rev. Mr. Tolles, Col. H. W. Wilson and others spoke for the remonstrants. Mr. Robinson made the closing argument for commutation, urging the insanity plea in all its possible phases for nearly two hours.

After the hearing no action was taken on the case until some time in June, when it is said that the vote of the Council was four in favor of commuting the sentence to five against. No action being taken by the Governor, Pomeroy remains in jail.

HIS ATTEMPT TO BREAK JAIL.

On Tuesday the 20th of July the officers of the prison discovered a very carefully matured plan by Pomeroy for his escape. He occupied a large cell, such as is used for the detention of debtors. It contained an iron bedstead, mattress and clothing, a hard wood chair, two buckets, a tin wash basin and an iron spoon. By some means he had removed the strong wire from the outer rim of the wash basin and with this, broken in several pieces, the cover of a sardine box and his iron spoon, he had removed the mortar from between the bricks sufficiently to enable him to take out several. His plan was discovered by one of the keepers who visited him abruptly and found a brick upon the floor. The mortar removed was concealed under his mattress. The place where he had been at work was concealed by paper pasted over it by means of soap.

Had he succeeded in piercing the wall and making his way into the corridor, he would still have found numerous bolts, bars and walls between himself and freedom, and it is impossible that he should have accomplished his purpose and made his escape. It was a foolish, boyish effort to gain his liberty, without danger to any one except himself, as the event has proved. He is now placed in a secure cell and more carefully watched and secluded.

CPSIA information can be obtained
at www.ICGtesting.com
Printed in the USA
LVHW101710081120
671079LV00025B/132